Social Philosophy Research Institute Book Series No. 1

WAR CRIMES AND LAWS OF WAR

Second Edition

Donald A. Wells

UNIVERSITY
PRESS OF
AMERICA

Lanham • New York • London

Copyright © 1984, 1991 by
University Press of America®, Inc.
4720 Boston Way
Lanham, Maryland 20706

3 Henrietta Street
London WC2E 8LU England

First edition copyright © 1984 by University Press of America.
Second edition © 1991 by University Press of America.

Co-published by arrangement with the
North American Society for Social Philosophy

Library of Congress Cataloging-in-Publication Data

Wells, Donald A. (Donald Arthur), 1917-
War crimes and laws of war / Donald A. Wells. — second ed.
    p.   cm. — (Social Philosophy Research Institute
                book series: no. 1)
        Includes bibliographical references.
    1. War (International law)   2. War crimes.
            3. Military law—United States.
                I. Title.   II. Series.
    JX4511.W44   1990   341.6—dc20   90–11938 CIP

        ISBN 0–8191–7931-0 (alk. paper)
        ISBN 0–8191–7932–9 (pbk. :alk. paper)

To my wife June, co-worker for peace

Social Philosophy Research Institute Book Series
North American Society for Social Philosophy

ACKNOWLEDGEMENTS

The author gratefully acknowledges the support of the Social Philosophy Institute for its sponsorship and especially to Professor Robert Ginsberg, Editor of the Social Philosophy Research Institute Book Series, whose careful copyediting and helpful advice added immeasurably to the book's accuracy and style, to Sherry Amundson who skillfully formatted the manuscript into its final form, and to the Rockefeller Foundation for the time at Bellagio, Italy during the final stages of the first edition.

CONTENTS

FOREWORD

We are faced today with a situation without precedent. We have the ability to exterminate all hands, and small entities have the capacity to put the most muscular countries at unsupportable risk. A corollary to this is that there are no technical or military ways to forestall these capabilities. The solution rests solely on political, and therefore, in the deepest sense, on moral choices.

While some *ex post facto* enforcement has been attempted, and even succeeded, as at Nuremberg and Tokyo, international law and its attendant legalisms have been overcome by the question of "Who is the judge?". All of this has been overwhelmed by the innovation of -- and the threat to use -- weapons of genocide indiscriminately against civilian populations. By their nature such weapons cannot sensibly be used in reprisal, for they threaten the existence of us all. These weapons and doctrines designed for genocide are the ultimate violation of the rules of war. Such technical innovations offer no answer. Ideology to defend the use of or the threat to use nuclear weapons serves only to fan the flames. It follows *inter alia* that we should renounce "first strike," which is simply a form of planned paranoia. It means also that we should renounce international terrorism in the indefensible practices of the CIA.

This book clearly states the evolution of the laws of war and of the attempts of civilization to put limits to barbarism. Donald Wells causes us to think on these matters which are nothing less than the future of mankind. The author has probed into the deep issues of war and morality. He has shown the conflicts, humane and political, in policies of death and destruction justified by appeals to "national defense." Most of all he has shown that the right track to survival with freedom does not lie in technology or military ruthlessness, but in political choices -- in the deepest sense, moral choices.

Admiral Noel Gayler U.S. Navy (Ret.)
Former Commander-in-Chief U.S. Pacific Forces
Sometime Director National Security Agency

PREFACE

The ability to identify crimes of war, crimes against humanity, and crimes against the peace depends upon the existence of rules or laws of war. The premises on which the Nuremberg and Tokyo Trials were held after World War II were based on a conviction that laws existed to make such conduct truly crimes and that international sentiment supported the Trials. The judges at Nuremberg and Tokyo believed that war crimes had been identified by the resolutions of The Hague Congresses of 1899 and 1907; that crimes against humanity had been specified by congresses of the International Red Cross at Geneva; and that crimes against the peace had been named by the Paris Peace Pact of 1928. Unfortunately, international jurists, though favoring the Trials, doubted that any international laws of war existed. The resolutions of congresses at The Hague and Geneva could be endorsed or rejected by nations to suit their perceived national interests, and in wars with non-signators even signator nations were relieved of any obligation to comply. Assurance that international law had been enhanced by the Trials received a setback when the General Assembly of the United Nations refused to ratify a proposal of the U.N. Commission on the Codification of International Law to formulate principles derivable from the Nuremberg precedent. The General Assembly also rejected a report of the same Commission which stated the nature of aggressive war and crimes against the peace.

Among the reasons for this general failure to adopt resolutions to curb the indiscriminate havoc of war are three military doctrines: military necessity, the right of reprisal, and the obligation of soldiers to obey superior orders without question. These doctrines supported the basic premise that sovereign nations had the right to wage wars in their national self-interest, and they created an historic dilemma. On the one hand, nations did not wish to lose their sovereignty over humanitarian concerns, yet, on the other hand, they did not wish to appear as callous brutes. Citizens wanted to believe that some acts of war were absolutely forbidden on moral grounds. The charges at Nuremberg assumed this was the case. The contrast between what these international congresses prohibited and what military manuals allowed set an unresolved conflict which it is the intent of this volume to pursue.

In the years since the first edition it has become evident that several of these matters were insufficiently considered. This edition has added a section on the importance of "just war" theory in setting the parameters of acceptable violence appealed to by the Congresses. The section on "May All Soldiers Be Slain?" has been amplified in the context of the apparent lack of rules for the protection of prisoners of war and an even greater failure to support a combatant-non-combatant distinction. The sections on whether there are forbidden strategies or weapons have been expanded to elaborate on the indiscriminate use of incendiaries, poison gases and noxious chemicals, biological warfare, and genocidal nuclear weapons. The long failure of the United States to approve the Genocide Convention has been documented.

If we were to cast all the post-Nuremberg stones at crimes of war, the list would be exceedingly long. It is not the intent of the author to catalogue such a list, helpful as this might be. We shall concentrate on America and on the American Army manuals, not because we are the chief offenders, but because this is where we are and this is where our influence can best be made. The premise of Nuremberg was that crimes of war could be named and as a participant in those Trials we can ill afford to dismiss them as instances of mere victor's justice. We need to avoid the acts of war which destroy those values which we have traditionally taken pride in striving to preserve.

Donald A. Wells
Emeritus Professor of Philosophy
University of Hawaii at Hilo
1990

Chapter 1
THE RELATION OF WAR CRIMES
TO LAWS OF WAR

The ability to identify crimes of war, crimes against humanity, and crimes against the peace depends upon the existence of rules or laws of war. The Trials at Nuremberg and Tokyo had found those rules in congresses like those at Geneva, at The Hague, and in the Paris Peace Pact. The judges at those Trials felt sure enough that laws of war were to be found there that they sentenced capitally German and Japanese soldiers and civilians. But were these really laws of war? Did they qualify in international law as binding on nations? Unfortunately, the texts in international law gave little encouragement to the Nuremberg assumption that there were, or had ever been, laws of war. At the same time the civilian and military slaughter at camps like Belsen, Buchenwald, and Maidanek were so unprecedented in their scope and concentrated so fully on the killing of innocent civilians of all ages, that there was a general belief that if any rules or laws existed at all, they would forbid such slaughter.

Outrage against certain acts of war had existed since ancient times, although this anger was rarely directed other than at the enemy. National leaders prided themselves on their own sensibilities, and they were quick to accuse their neighbors of barbarity in war. The Athenians accused the Spartans of needless cruelties in war. Roman historians portrayed their enemies from the north as brutes. Early Christians, on the other hand, insisted that the Romans were without conscience in war, and Augustine claimed that when soldiers became Christians they would wage wars with humanity. Indeed, Augustine claimed, that the advent of Christianity had been an ameliorating force in all human relations.

This tendency to parade one's own virtues by denying such virtues to the enemy continued throughout history. Many American leaders in the twentieth century spoke of the Soviet Union the way the Athenians had spoken about Sparta. The Allied accusations about German atrocities in World War I commonly had little foundation in fact and implied that the Allies were far too virtuous to have done such deeds.

Writers of conviction from both the North and South during the Civil War in the United States had accused their opponents as lacking in humane sensitivities, while claiming for themselves the highest morality in war. Yet, quite apart from where the truth lay in these charges and countercharges an almost universal concern remained with rejecting certain acts of war. Accompanying this concern was an implicit assumption that the advancement of civilization made the continuation of such outrages insupportable. While no one expected battle deaths to be eliminated by some knightly code, it was hoped that the manner of the killing would become dignified by some rules of chivalry or fair play. There was little objection to what was considered to be the proper violence of war, but it was believed that moral limits applied to what soldiers should be allowed to do.

Unquestionably a mixture of genuine humane concern together with the traditional victor's pique prompted the Allies to announce in advance (1943) their intention to prosecute the Axis leaders for criminal acts of war. To implement this intention a Tribunal was selected to draw up a Charter which would contain the criminal charges. The atrocities committed in the concentration camps headed the list. The offenses there had been inflicted on prisoners of war or innocent civilians. By long tradition both of these groups had been assiduously protected from any acts of violence against them. It was not the intention of the Tribunal to indict war as such nor to prosecute soldiers who killed in the line of militarily necessary battle. By tradition a combatant-non-combatant distinction had been asserted, and the extermination camps had radically violated this.

SOLDIERS ARE NOT LIKE POLICE

There was some precedent, as we shall note, for conducting war crimes trials. The Allies had attempted to conduct such trials of the Germans after World War I. The Trial of Captain Henry Wirtz after the Civil War was a war crimes trial. The American Army had tried some of its own soldiers for putative war crimes following the Philippine War. Some precedent existed for presuming laws of war under which offenders would be duly prosecuted.

Unfortunately, the municipal laws of nations provided little precedent for an international trial, especially where the victorious nations served as judge and jury of the vanquished. In municipal courts of law the accused face a neutral judge, an equally impartial jury of their peers, and police who have arrested them. In addition a body of established laws existed which named the crimes in question and prescribed the punishment. These laws always antedated the offenses. Further, safeguards ensured some proportionality between the punishments and the offenses, and provisions were made for reconsideration in the event of a miscarriage of justice. In those places where there was no capital punishment such reconsideration was almost endlessly possible.

It was understood domestically, that police and citizens were engaged primarily in a non-deadly enterprise. It was understood that the laws gave protection for those engaged in pacific business. War did not parallel this situation in any sense. In war soldiers were professional killers who were assumed to be performing a legitimate task when they killed each other. In the domestic scene only the police were authorized to carry and to use weapons to kill, and ideally they were to shoot only to wound or disable. Whatever defense domestic criminals might offer, it was unthinkable that they could excuse their acts on the grounds that killing was their official business. The judges at Nuremberg were aware that no accused could be found guilty merely because they were paid killers, nor because they had in fact killed some persons. Indeed, until 1944 the U.S. Army manual, *Rules of Land Warfare*, exempted all soldiers of whatever nation for blame in following superior military orders even when such orders commanded soldiers to commit traditionally forbidden acts of slaughter against innocent civilians. In 1944, in anticipation of the war crimes trials to follow the end of the war, the United States changed the section on "superior orders" so that the following of orders was not an automatic excuse for otherwise heinous acts. Superiors, for their part, were expected to show some humanity, or at least awareness of laws of war, so that they did not give criminal orders. It was to be assumed that some parameters existed outside of which soldiers could be accused of crimes against humanity or war crimes. These parameters were, however, unclear as we shall see when we consider the question whether there are forbidden weapons or strategies. Unlike domestic police, soldiers were not required to shoot to wound rather than shoot to kill. Soldiers were allowed to use any force required until the enemy surrendered. "Humanity" and "chivalry," which the Army manual asserted conditioned military necessity, apparently applied only to acts against soldiers *hors de combat* and civilian slaughter not militarily necessary.

This blanket of protection for the individual soldiers had been clearly affirmed in the 1940 edition of *Rules of Land Warfare*. Soldiers could not be punished for war acts when they were following superior orders. The officers who gave the orders, however, might be disciplined for having given orders against the "laws of war." Soldiers of every country, regardless of its political persuasion, were considered to be patriots as they fired their rifles, hurled grenades, aimed their flame throwers, or dropped their bombs. As professionals they were entitled to certain on-the-job protections. The new revision merely required officers and rank-and-file soldiers to justify the orders they gave or obeyed. Since every enemy soldier, except for those *hors de combat*, deserved to be slain whenever doing so would aid the war effort, soldiers would not be prosecuted for killing soldiers no matter in what numbers. Even so-called innocent bystanders might become proper targets wherever the right of reprisal or military necessity warranted. Domestic police, on the other hand, could not justify destroying a neighborhood on the grounds that to do so would assist them in the capture of sought after criminals. The kinds of weapons issued to police as compared with soldiers further indicated no significant parallels. Police did not receive flame throwers, fragmentation bombs, nor an air force equipped with nuclear explosives. Soldiers were not simply international police, nor was war merely the prosecution of domestic crime on a larger scale.

Another sense in which any analogy between soldiers and police was inapplicable was in the area of laws or rules. The actions of the police were strictly limited as they attempted to apprehend criminals or prevent crimes. Under no circumstances could police justify killing bystanders even if to do so would aid the police in the capture of some criminal. Soldiers operated under no such limitations. While plunder and rapine were generally prohibited no limit seemed to apply to the amount of civilian destruction soldiers could inflict if to do so would be militarily effective. Even the medieval mandate against shelling unfortified cities, or against attacking a city occupied by civilians without first warning of the attack so that the civilians could flee, had exceptions. Given the right conditions commanders could wage an attack of "no quarter" and kill every man, woman, and child. Even the current U.S. Army manual, *The Law of Land Warfare*, permitted the most devastating bombing against basically civilian targets. This general indifference to what happened to civilians was in contrast to a traditional concern for what happened to soldiers who were *hors de combat*, wounded, or prisoners of war. *General Orders 100*, issued in 1863 as the first American Army manual, was to be used as a guidebook for soldiers in the field. It proposed that hospitals and prisoner of war camps be considered as "safe zones" and that they be spared any direct assaults in battle. On the battlefield, however, and against able-bodied soldiers no limit seemed to apply to what soldiers could do to each other. In considering a war crimes trial, therefore, little precedent appeared for guidance from domestic law courts.

THE SEARCH FOR RULES

Given the nature of modern weapons and strategies of war it was not easy for the Nuremberg court to determine when a soldier had committed a crime. Now, a generation after those Trials, it is even less easy to do so. General Telford Taylor observed this at the time of the Nuremberg Trials.

> War consists largely of acts that would be criminal if performed in time of peace -- killing, wounding, kidnapping, destroying or carrying off other people's property. Such conduct is not regarded as criminal if it takes place in the course of war, because the state of war lays a blanket of immunity over the warriors.[1]

Indeed, this immunity had no counterpart in any analogy with domestic police. American soldiers could "destroy a city in order to save it." Police, on the other hand, could not destroy a single city street no matter what the threat might be from the criminal element. The only way the Allies could prosecute the German and Japanese was to establish that this "blanket of immunity" had limits. The first task was to provide a legal basis for such a claim. This required that the judges be able to name the rules or laws of war from which these limits could be derived.

From a variety of sources such laws might be deduced or induced. Reference to rules or laws of war were at least as ancient as the time of Thucydides. In the Middle Ages the rules of knighthood added to a storehouse of sentiment in favor of rules of war. The Peace of God and the Truce of God formalized some of these rules. Roman Catholic Church Councils issued mandates against the use of incendiaries, poisons, or the crossbow. Obviously, non-Christians would not feel religiously compelled to follow such advice. More importantly, however, Christian soldiers found such rules to be obstacles to military success and tended to modify such "rules" with their doctrine of "military necessity."

From the sixteenth through the eighteenth centuries a group of jurists attempted to formulate some international laws of war. They intended, essentially, to base what conclusions they could on the facts of customs of war, which were widely enough practiced so that it could be said a rule or law existed. Although by the nineteenth century writers of international law texts doubted that custom was sufficiently widespread to warrant the claim of laws of war, both the language and the issues raised by these international legal jurists set the parameters of what to hope for should laws of war ever be agreed to.

Just war theory as developed by St. Ambrose, St. Augustine, and St. Thomas contributed significantly to the substance of the international dialogue concerning laws or rules of war. Their assertion that wars needed to be just in both their ends and means gave rise to serious attention to the means or methods by which wars were fought. They contributed the notion that the means of war ought not to be disproportional to the ends of war. They insisted that there should be protected persons in war and this became the important "combatant-non-combatant" distinction. These thinkers believed that laws of war could not be based simply on what had been custom. Customs varied, and that the crimes of the past could become the virtues of the future was a real risk. The Roman Catholic theologians based their arguments on natural law theory. According to this the rules of war were not simply national customs, but rested instead on universal laws derived from divine laws. But once the Roman Empire became fractured into warring Christian states, the resulting lack of unanimity as to what was natural in war, and was universal, or divine, undermined the entire basis of natural law. The philosophical and theological arguments of these just war theorists rested on a view of natural law and divine law which has long since faded into obscurity. Nonetheless the belief that there are important questions of justice with regard to the ways in which wars are waged persisted, and the Nuremberg courts had occasion to appeal to some such notions of justice and injustice. The rise of nationalism led to the general abandonment of concern with whether a war was just in its ends. Waging war was a national right, and consequently every nation always had justice on its side, in the absence of any international body to determine otherwise.

The period of the Roman Catholic Church inquisitions proved a boon to the doctrine of military necessity and a serious setback for the hope that limits could be set to what could be done in war. The Spanish inquisitors had argued that the importance of eternal salvation justified seriousness in the punishment for sin. This seriousness on the part of the Church leaders corresponded with the seriousness with which the military viewed victory. Thus, in the inquisition, as in war, once it was granted that the obstinate could be justly killed, it was not possible to indict either spiritual or military leaders solely on the grounds that they had caused suffering or death. War makers, like inquisitors, saw the stakes as being ultimately important. For both there was a fate worse than death. Commitment to the thesis of sovereign nationalism did for the justification of war what belief in eternal salvation had done for the justification of the inquisition.

Another source for the claim that rules or laws of war existed were the military manuals written for the guidance of soldiers in battle. These were of two very different sorts. On the one hand, and by far the oldest kind of manual, were those which dealt with rules or laws within a given army. The current *Universal Code of Military Justice* of the United States forces is of this type. Its aim is to keep some sense of order within the ranks, to maintain the hierarchical chain of command, and to ensure obedience to orders given. A custom bearing on this concern for obedience was typified in an ordinance of King Richard I in 1190 that,

> Whoever shall slay a man on shipboard, he shall be bound to the dead man and thrown into the sea.[2]

The early Hindu *Code of Manu* in the sixth century B.C. was an instance of the other type of manual which directed attention to affairs between armies. In that manual leaders of state were advised that,

> When the king fights with his foes in battle, let him not strike with weapons concealed in wood, nor with such as arrows barbed, poisoned or the points of which are blazing fire.[3]

The United States Army produced the first "international" manual during the Civil War. It appeared in 1863 under the title, *General Orders 100: Instructions for the Armies of the United States in the Field.* This manual was written by Professor Francis Lieber of Columbia College at the request of Secretary of War Stanton and with the approval of President Lincoln. President Lincoln had copies distributed to the officers of both the Union and Confederate armies. This manual inspired similar efforts by the armies of Spain, Germany, and France, who cited from it almost verbatim. It was quoted at congresses on war both at Geneva and The Hague. This U.S. Army manual was revised in 1914, 1934, 1940, 1944, 1956, and 1976. Citations in all editions made reference to the existence of laws or rules of war and warned that infractions of these rules would carry penalties.

At the recommendation of Professor Lieber in a letter to Mr. Rolyn-Jacquemyns, editor of the *Revue de Droit Internationale*, an Institute of International Law was established. It held its first meeting in Geneva in 1874. In his annual report of 1878 Rolyn-Jacquemyns, then the Secretary-General of the Institute, recommended a study of the codes used by other nations to advise their armies. Gustave Moynier was given the task of research, and in 1880 he submitted a draft of a code which relied heavily on Lieber's manual. While his draft was accepted at the meeting of the Institute in 1880 at Oxford University, for obvious reasons the delegates chose to have their respective nations draft their own codes for advice.

The emphasis in *General Orders 100*, and in all subsequent revisions was upon the treatment of prisoners of war, soldiers *hors de combat* by reason of their wounds, and civilians exposed to the violence of battle. All these manuals assumed that nations had the right to go to war in their perceived national interest and to continue such war until victory. No provisions were ever made for rules that might seriously hinder the military objectives. Three military doctrines guided all advice: the right of reprisal, the obligation of soldiers to obey orders given by their superiors, and the ultimate appeal to be allowed to do whatever was militarily necessary.

The weightiest sources to which the Nuremberg Tribunal appealed as bases for rules or laws of war were the major peace congresses at The Hague in 1899 and 1907 and the series of International Red Cross sponsored congresses in Geneva beginning in 1864 and continuing through 1906 and 1929. The conventions issued at the two Hague congresses were believed to be the basis for laws of war which gave the evidence that war crimes could exist. The conventions issued at the International Red Cross meetings were appealed to as the source of the charge that crimes against humanity could occur. The Paris Peace Pact of 1928 was cited as evidence that "crimes against the peace" could exist. The current U.S. Army manual, *The Law of Land Warfare,* and Army pamphlet 27-1, *Treaties Governing Land Warfare,* both contain a list of three Hague conventions and four Geneva conventions to which the United States Army considers itself bound. The 1976 revision of *The Law of Land Warfare* added the Geneva Protocol of 1925 concerning the use of gas and noxious chemicals, although the manual reserved the U.S. right to interpret which gases and chemicals were to be included in the 1925 Protocol. In contrast to this American commitment, the *British Manual of Military Law: The Law of War on Land,* Part III listed in addition to the three Hague conventions and the four Geneva conventions accepted by the United States, three further Hague declarations from the 1899 session and one from the 1907 session, the Geneva Protocol of 1925 minus the U.S. reservations, the Genocide Convention of the United Nations, and a 1954 Geneva Convention not on the American shorter list.[4] Yet even this list was shorter than that to which the Nuremberg judges appealed.

The major textbooks on international law support these Nuremberg inferences: that The Hague supplies us with evidence for the charge of war crimes, and that Geneva gives evidence for the charge of crimes against humanity. The major thrust of The Hague findings was to establish that non-belligerents should be protected, that prisoners of war should be cared for, and that limits apply to both strategy and weapons in war.[5] The Geneva conventions concentrated on protection of civilians, soldiers who were wounded or in prison, and those doctors and nurses who treated them.[6] *The Law of Land Warfare* notes these two emphases and gives the impression that some way exists to reconcile the demands of military necessity with these concerns.[7] What we need to determine is whether and to what degree the doctrine of military necessity takes precedence over these Hague and Geneva limitations. The U.S. Army manual states that armies may use all force necessary for victory, subject to the requirements of "humanity" and "chivalry." What limits do "humanity" and "chivalry" impose? Did the accused Germans act inhumanely or unchivalrously, or did they perform militarily unnecessary war acts? It was not coincidental that the American delegates to The Hague assigned to determine the amount of permissible force were all professional military officers, and that they voted against most of the conventions.[8]

U.S. ARMY MANUALS AND PEACE DECLARATIONS

The friction between the American Army manuals and the declarations of the peace congresses has been reflected in the standard texts on international law. A comment by W.E. Hall in 1880 was typical of the prevailing view.

> International law has no alternative but to accept war, independently of the justice of its origin. Hence, both parties to every war are regarded as being in an identical legal position, and consequently as being possessed of equal rights.[9]

This position was reaffirmed in the twentieth century by the international jurist, Charles G. Fenwick.

> On the eve of the first World War the principle that there must be a 'just cause of war' had practically disappeared from the treatises of the jurists.[10]

The distinguished jurist, L. Oppenheim, observed that confusion had been generated by the Nuremberg Tribunal's appeal to the Paris Pact as having outlawed war. If war had been outlawed, he noted, then there would be no reason to have laws of war at all. If war was forbidden, it would be inconsistent to claim that rules still existed. He noted, further, the general sentiment in favor of denying to belligerents any protection at all from laws of war. Yet, he cautioned,

> At the same time in view of the humanitarian character of a substantial part of the rule of war it is imperative that during the war these rules should be mutually observed regardless of the legality of the war.[11]

We can appreciate the comments of the British jurist, John Austin, when he concluded that international laws lack the basic ingredients of law. No sanctions existed for obeying them, there was no court for the adjudication of offenses against them, and nations could, therefore, choose not to obey them at all. In addition, domestic law presupposes legal inferiors and superiors, whereas in war no such relationship was believed to exist. When Austin considered these defects of so-called laws of war, he relegated them to the domain of "positive morality."[12]

These defects were evident in the pronouncements of The Hague Congresses. The findings of The Hague allowed that non-signators were not bound to obey, and in wars with non-signators, even signators were relieved of compliance with the declarations. *The Law of Land Warfare*, for example, dismissed The Hague prohibition against dropping projectiles from balloons, with the comment that the prohibition "is said to be of comparatively slight value."[13] Indeed, the value was so slight that laws governing aerial warfare remained virtually non-existent even though the most serious devastation of war came from aerial troops. The manual, *The Law of Land Warfare,* stated further that The Hague provisions against the use of gases and chemicals did not apply to any of the gases and chemicals in the United States arsenals.[14] The manual asserted, further, that The Hague conventions against weapons which caused "unnecessary suffering" or "superfluous injury" were merely intended to prohibit needlessly excessive weapons. The criterion of excess was military rather than humanitarian. At the outbreak of World War II the only weapons listed in the U.S. Army manual as banned as excessive for American troops were the same ones listed in the nineteenth century manual, namely, lances with barbed tips, projectiles filled with glass, and bullets dipped in irritants.[15]

The problem may be simply put. There are war crimes, if and only if, there are laws of war. There are crimes against humanity, if and only if, there are humanitarian laws. There are crimes against the peace, if and only if, there are laws against going to war at all. Furthermore, such laws require a neutral adjudicating agency. Some sanction compelling compliance must exist. Customs of war, however widespread, were always changed under the demands of military exigency. In addition, the "right of reprisal" permitted soldiers to commit otherwise improper acts with impunity. Were some neutral court available to assess the genuine military necessities or to weigh the relative importance of the demands of humanity and chivalry, the problems of courts prosecuting for war crimes might not be so unresolvable. Unfortunately, military necessity is always measured by the respective armies committing the acts in question. The Allies determined that dropping the atomic bombs on Hiroshima and Nagasaki was militarily warranted while the Axis deeds in the extermination camps were not.

Proportionality was an extremely important criterion derived from just war theories of St. Augustine and St. Thomas. The task was to provide a yardstick to measure when the violence of the means was proportional to the importance of ends to be preserved. The Nuremberg courts ruled that the deeds of the Germans and Japanese were excessive, while the courts failed to provide a measure of what a proper amount of violence would be. Pope Innocent III indicted the crossbow as excessive, and this gave the medieval Christian soldier some idea of how important the ends of war were compared with the violence of the means. Pope John XXIII did not level the judgment of excessiveness until he came to nuclear bombs. Short of these mega-weapons, the Pope accepted chemical warfare, aerial bombing, and flame throwers as not excessive. Under this circumstance the modern Catholic soldier could not have the faintest idea how modern ends had become so much more important than the medieval ones which had led to the prohibition against the crossbow.

The answers to these questions were crucial if any war crimes trials were to be justified. Without answers there would be no way to argue that Nuremberg set any viable precedent. Little doubt was evident on the part of the Nuremberg Tribunals that the extermination camps were excessive, or that they served no viable military purpose. After all, conventional weapons like flame throwers, napalm, fragmentation bombs, chemical/biological agents, and bombs with non-nuclear explosives were far more destructive than anything imagined by medieval just war theorists. How could the Nuremberg judges rule against the camps yet in favor of the rest of conventional warfare? The Nuremberg and Tokyo Trials hoped to resolve these matters in a context which still retained the right of reprisal and the doctrine of military necessity. With respect to the argument used by the defendants that their acts were proper reprisals, the judges needed to show that no prior offenses had been committed. With respect to military necessity, the courts needed to show that the extermination camps served no pressing military need. Perhaps they also needed establish that such acts were so barbaric that they could not be defended even where military necessity was shown.

Over a generation has passed since those landmark Trials. The parameters of military deeds covered by military necessity have increased prodigiously. Weapons of war and the strategies which they allow have become more lethal and less discriminating. The traditional distinction between combatants and non-combatants seems to have vanished. Can we still argue for legal limits beyond which war ought not to go? Has modern war moved to a point beyond the possibility of there being rules of war? This is not simply a question of whether war can be humanized, important as that question may be. It is, rather, whether war crimes, crimes against humanity, or crimes against the peace can even be identified, given the blanket of immunity which covers the military enterprise under the shield of military necessity. We shall trace first the sources of those customs of war which were deemed in the past to provide rules of war to determine whether any hope remains that they will enable us to make present or future accusations of war criminality. We shall consider, further, whether past efforts to set limits to war making support the results of Nuremberg and give bases for renewed efforts to set limits to what should be justified in war.

NOTES

1. Telford Taylor, *Nuremberg and Vietnam: An American Tragedy* (New York: Time Books, 1970), p. 19.

2. William B. Aycock and Seymour W. Wurfel, *Military Law Under the Uniform Code of Military Justice* (Chapel Hill: University of North Carolina Press, 1955), p. 3.

3. Cited in Paul A. Roblee, Jr., "The Legitimacy of Modern Conventional Weaponry," *Military Law Review*, Vol. 71 (Winter, 1976), p. 99.

4. *The Law of War on Land*. Part III of the *Manual of Military Law*. Issued by command of the Army Council (London: Her Majesty's Stationery Office, 1958).

5. Jean Pictet, *The Principles of International Humanitarian Law* (Geneva: International Committee of the Red Cross, 1966), p. 32.

6. *Ibid.*

7. *The Law of Land Warfare*, Section I.

8. Cf. Colonel G.I.A. Draper, "The Ethical and Juridical Status of Restraints in War," *Military Law Review*, Vol. 55 (Winter, 1972).

9. Cited in J.L. Brierly, *The Law of Nations* (Oxford: Oxford University Press, 1963), p. 398.

10. Charles G. Fenwick, *International Law* (New York: Appleton-Century-Crofts, 1948), p. 542.

11. L. Oppenheim, *International Law*, Vol. II. 7th edit. H. Lauterpacht (ed.) (New York: Longmans, 1952), pp. 217-218.

12. Fenwick, *International Law*, p. 38.

13. *The Law of Land Warfare* (Washington: The U.S. Government Printing Office, 1956), paragraph 27.

14. *Ibid.*, paragraph 29.

15. *Ibid.*, paragraph 34.

Chapter 2
JUST WAR THEORY
AND THE MILITARY TRADITION

Historically it was presupposed that the waging of war was a right of sovereign states by which they preserved their country from attack, extended their empire, came to the defense of their friends, and punished their enemies. As a consequence, early criticisms of war making were not against its use in principle, but voiced opposition when the ends were unworthy or the means were excessive. The word "just" was utilized in such judgments. Aristotle (384-322 B.C.) had observed that,

> The art of war is a natural acquisition, for the art of acquisition includes hunting, an art which we ought to practice against wild beasts, and against men who, though intended by nature to be governed, will not submit; for war of such a kind is naturally just.[1]

Cicero (106-43 B.C.) urged that the laws of war be obeyed so that men might be better than brutes in their war making. He reminded his contemporaries that war was a human enterprise, and that it ought, therefore, to be amenable to humanizing laws. He had concluded that wars for property and for glory were just wars, although those for conquest or national glory alone should be carried out with a minimum of hatred.[2]

The first serious effort to apply humane criteria to the practices of war was made by St. Ambrose (334-397) and his distinguished pupil, St. Augustine (354-430). Until Constantine had adopted Christianity as the official religion of the Roman Empire, Christians had generally ignored the role of soldiers in war as they also ignored the role of politicians, teachers, leaders of business, lawyers, and the like. These writers felt called upon to explain how the new religion considered war making. Augustine's general thesis was that the advent of Christianity had brought an ameliorating effect into Roman life.

15

All the spoiling, then, which Rome was exposed to in the recent calamity, all the slaughter, plundering, burning and misery, was the result of the custom of war. But what was novel, was that savage barbarians showed themselves in so gentle a guise, that the largest churches were chosen and set apart for the purpose of being filled with the people to whom quarter was given, and in them none were slain..... Whoever does not see that this is to be attributed to the name of Christ, and to the Christian temper is blind.... Far be it from any prudent man to impute this clemency to the barbarians.[3]

Augustine presumed that Christian soldiers, although participating in the killing, did so with more grace, more reserve, less malice, less needless destruction, and for a worthier cause. Little biblical evidence existed for this presumption. The Old Testament Pentateuch was too filled with bloody tales of indiscriminate war, all with the claimed support of Jehovah, for there to be scriptural reasons for expecting Christian war to be any improvement over heathen war. When it came to winning the Promised Land, nothing appeared to be rejected as excessive by the zealous Jews if the chances for victory would be increased. The faithful in Psalm 137 were urged by Jehovah to dash the heads of the Edomite children on the rocks of the city wall. This prayerful vengeance was even more difficult to reconcile with charity, considering that the Edomites were cousins to the Jews through Esau. Indeed, *Isaiah* 13:1-19 could plead for the abandonment of war and the beating of swords into plowshares, and still predict that Jehovah would wreak his vengeance on Babylon similar to what he had done in Sodom and Gomorrah. In these latter cases this had included killing babies, ravishing women, and the disembowelling of pregnant women.

Augustine dealt both with the just reasons for declaring and waging a war, and with the just means for conducting it. With regard to the first matter Augustine insisted that the war had to be declared by the duly constituted authority. This authority was secular since the notion of a papacy did not appear for another four centuries. This principle effectively silenced the citizens from criticizing the propriety of any war declared by the emperor. Secondly, the war needed a worthy or just cause. The ends which satisfied this criterion were basically those which motivated secular leaders of state in the first place: namely, to extend empire, to defend the empire from attack, to punish enemies, and to come to the aid of one's friends.[4] A third criterion touched on both the ends and means of war, that the intentions had to be "rightful." He remarked in this regard,

> True religion looks upon as peaceful those wars that are waged not from motives of aggrandizement or cruelty, but with the object of securing peace, of punishing evil-doers, and of uplifting the good.[5]

If it was unjust to wage wars for the wrong reasons and with the wrong intentions, the problem then, as now, was to determine what those occasions were where wrong reason ruled and when the intentions were worthy enough to justify the slaughter of war. Since duly constituted authorities judged their own motives, such a criterion was really empty.

These matters received further attention by Roman Catholic Church Councils which issued declarations concerning proper weapons, proper strategies, and proper targets. At one such Council, the Synod of Charroux in 989 proclaimed:

> Anathema against those who injure clergymen. If anyone attacks, seizes or beats a priest, deacon, or any other clergyman, who is not bearing arms (shield, sword, coat of mail, or helmet), but is going along peacefully or staying in the house, the sacrilegious person shall be excommunicated and cut off from the church, unless he makes satisfaction, or unless a bishop discovers that the clergyman brought it on himself.[6]

The major elements in modern notions of laws of war are present in this proclamation. The combatant-non-combatant distinction was drawn, and the sense of limits to what soldiers should be permitted to do was present. This idea that innocents should be spared was reasserted in later Church Councils. The Second Lateran Council of 1139 listed the penalties for violating the rules for the protection of these non-combatants. The Council declared also that slings should be outlawed and incendiaries forbidden.[7] Pope Innocent III proposed the banning of the use of the crossbow on the grounds that it caused needless suffering and was too excessive to be justified by any conceivable end.

These efforts to set limits to justifiable war faced an equally vigorous campaign by military writers who rejected any attempt to set limits on the mere grounds of humanitarian sentiment. To some degree these military mandates had support from the church traditions in the inquisitions. After all, churchmen had urged their followers, "Thou shalt make war against the infidel without cessation and without mercy."[8] These military counsels came to their zenith in the *Policraticus* of John of Salisbury. In 1159 he dedicated his book to Thomas Beckett in whose service he had worked for ten years prior to the latter's death. In the tradition of the two sword theory, one papal and the other secular, John linked military service on a par with religious obligation. Obedience to the king in battle was equated with obedience to God.

> Turn over in your mind the words of the oath itself, and you will find that the soldiery of arms not less than the spiritual soldiery is bound by the requirements of its official duties to the sacred service and worship of God; for they owe obedience to the prince and ever-watchful service to the commonwealth loyally and according to God.[9]

John established a connection between religious and military obligation which has remained to the present time, and is reflected at least in the role of the military chaplain. Like clergymen, soldiers are ordained to their offices.

> But what is the office of the duly ordained soldiery? To defend the Church, to assail infidelity, to venerate the priesthood, to protect the poor from injuries, to pacify the province, to pour out their blood for their brothers, and, if need be, to lay down their lives.[10]

Unlike their spiritual brothers, the service of soldiers was given independently of the worthiness of the cause. For this reason the emphasis upon obeying superior orders was important as a legal protection for the soldier who might be asked to do in war what would be a punishable offense in peacetime. Soldiers were morally neutral and justice was a foreign word. John asserted:

> It makes no difference whether a soldier serves one of the faithful or an infidel, so long as he serves without impairing or violating his own faith.[11]

Since the soldier's faith consisted of obedience to higher authority, much as did the religious devotee, the chief impairment a soldier might suffer would be if he questioned superior orders. Conflict was potential between the declarations of Church Councils banning certain weapons or strategies on religious grounds of justice and the blind commitment of the soldier to the orders of his military superior.

Were there no limits to what soldiers might do while carrying out their duties? John dealt with this question in a chapter titled, "That Soldiers Are to Be Punished with Severity if in Contempt of Military Laws They Abuse Their Privileges." What might these contemptible acts be, and what were the punishments prescribed? A first prohibition was against theft and rapine. Soldiers guilty of such deeds would be punished more severely than non-soldiers in view of the fact that military men were professionals.[12] Other proscribed acts for soldiers were luxurious living, intemperance, disobedience, and lack of discipline. Under some circumstances of disobedience a soldier might suffer loss of pay, banishment to Sicily, or barley rations for up to seven years. Soldiers might be reduced in rank. Cowardice was often punished by opening a vein and drawing an excessive amount of blood. What if the superior commanded the soldier to commit theft or rapine? John's position was clear.

> In the military there must be no questioning of the commander's orders by the soldier....In such matters it is a crime even to blink an eye save at the commander's bidding....He that is under obligation must be blind on this side as a condition of living....If you bid me plunge my sword in my brother's heart or my father's throat, or into the womb of my wife big with child, I will do in full your bidding, though with an unwilling hand.[13]

Raymond of Penafort (1176-1275), Canon of Barcelona, and an enthusiastic supporter of the Crusades and the Inquisitions, asserted five elements to a just war.

- The war must be fought by laymen. Priests were forbidden to take up arms.

- The aim of the war must be to redress some wrong committed against rights, possessions, or persons.

- The war must be a last resort.

- The aim of those who fight must be a genuine desire for peace.

- The war must be authorized by the Roman Catholic Church or by a sovereign prince.[14]

Like the writers of his time Raymond assumed that wars for national defense needed no justification. Raymond assessed the fifth element as the most important. This followed from the fact that the duly constituted authorities were the ones to establish that the other four elements were satisfied.

St. Thomas (1225-1275) revived the Augustinian criteria in the context of four questions about war.[15] First, "Whether some kind of war is lawful?" His answer was that just wars were lawful and that to be just three conditions needed to be met:

o   The war must be declared by the duly constituted authority.

o   There must be a just cause.

o   The belligerents must have just intentions. This third condition might have prompted Thomas to comment on excesses in war and proportionality in means, but he made no mention of these matters. Instead he cited St. Augustine's remark to the effect that if the war is just it doesn't matter what means are used.

The only comments Thomas made about violence were in the context of jousting, and the point was that such manly exercises were not forbidden provided that they were not "inordinate and perilous."[16] He remarked that soldiers ought not to have a "passion for inflicting harm" but this referred to intentions, not to the amount of violence.[17] While Christians were to slay their enemies with charity, this did not appear to entail any moderation.[18]

His second question was "Whether it is lawful for clerics to fight?" He concluded that it was not, because soldiering hindered the mind from the full contemplation of the Eucharist. Furthermore, the sacred host ought not to be handled by persons who had shed blood. This was a sacramental not a moral matter.

The third question was, "Whether it is lawful to lay ambushes?" Again paraphrasing Augustine, Thomas remarked that in just wars the methods of war were of no concern.[19]

The fourth question was, "Whether it is lawful to fight on holy days?" The answer was a simple affirmative, thus nullifying the Truces of the past which had forbidden wars on certain holy days. Thomas observed that if medical doctors could help their patients on any day, surely the soldiers who held the health of the commonwealth in their hands could do so also.[20]

Thomas's writings added little to the questions relating to whether limits existed to what soldiers were permitted to do. Such matters, Thomas maintained, were properly left to civil authorities. In his essay on "Princely Government," he concluded

> It is a king's duty to make sure that the community subject
> to him is made safe from its enemies. There is no point in
> guarding against internal danger when defense from enemies
> without is impossible.[21]

Perhaps the fact that three of the nine Crusades were carried out in
Thomas's lifetime, with the support of Pope Innocent IV and the
Council of Lyon, accounted for his failure to express moral concern for
wanton killing, contemporary Christian conscientious objectors to such
killing, or the shabby reasons or ends for which most wars of the time
were being fought. Indeed, one century later, Giovanni da Legnano
(died 1383), Professor of Canon Law at the University of Bologna, had
barely moved beyond the crusade mentality. He still justified wars of
the church against infidels and any wars declared by the Emperor. He
made no mention of the possibility that some wars might be unworthy
even though they were properly declared. Wars by Christians against
infidels were always just. These were called "Roman Wars". Wars to
curb the rebellious or to repel invaders were called "necessary wars."
He did not discuss excesses nor did he name any so-called law of
war.[22]

Just war theory succumbed to military reservations throughout its
long history. In part this was inevitable since most just war theorists
were apologists for their respective states, and they seemed unwilling
to challenge their military contemporaries. Yet, just war theorists raised
important issues even if they did not confront those issues adequately.
Just war theory provided the potential of parameters of proportionality
of means to ends, the importance of the ends for which wars are
fought, and the combatant-non-combatant distinction.[23] The major
contribution in establishing rules or laws of war was made by a series
of international jurists of the sixteenth through the eighteenth centuries
whom we shall now consider.

WHO MAY PROPERLY DECLARE WAR?

Franciscus de Victoria deduced from natural law theory that all
states as self-governing bodies had certain rights with respect to war.
Indeed, with regard to defensive war, where a country has been
invaded, even private citizens could enter a conflict without further
warrant. He remarked, "Anyone can make this kind of war, without
authority from anyone else."[24] With respect to offensive war, every
nation had the right to declare it and to wage it. In the case of war
between dukes, where a king had neglected to resolve some dispute,
"The aggrieved city may not only resort to self-defense, but may also
commence war."[25] Yet, even though the duly constituted authority had

the right to declare and wage war, not every reason for doing so was justifiable. He particularly rejected wars for religion, for the personal glory of the prince, or for the extension of empire. Indeed, he rejected the prevailing papal view that faith did not need to be kept with heretics and unbelievers. He introduced the genesis of the doctrine of military necessity and the obligation of soldiers to obey superior orders. He depersonalized the role of the soldier so that the soldier was relieved from moral responsibility. Some acts of war were, thereby, immune from condemnation.

Pierino Belli (1502-1575) began his treatise on military matters with the same assumption, that all nations had the same right to wage wars. He observed,

> More briefly it is my view that any people or nation living under its own laws and its own charges, and any king or ruler who is fully independent, may declare war at will and when the occasion arises.[26]

He granted that the Pope had the clear right to declare war, and he urged lesser prelates to get papal approval.

Balthazar Ayala (1548-1584) said that while private persons could not on their own begin a war, yet if their prince was absent and if great hazards would ensue if they were to wait for his return, the people could go to war immediately.

Francisco Suarez (1548-1617) spoke of defensive wars of a preventive nature, a precursor to the modern view of "first strike." A nation could fire the first shot and still be considered to be waging a defensive war. He accepted alliances between Christian princes and non-Christian ones, and he gave early assent to the premise that the justice of a war did not depend upon the ideology of those who waged it. Who were these authoritative rulers who could declare war? They were those with no superior over them.[27] Under an aggressive papacy, only the Pope could declare war. From this he concluded that any war,

> declared without legitimate authority, is contrary not only to charity, but also to justice, even if a legitimate cause for it exists.[28]

Hugo Grotius (1583-1645) reaffirmed the importance of having the proper authority declare the war.[29] He added the admonition to princes that some wars would be unjust for them to wage.[30] Unlike Suarez he rejected the idea of preventive war, although he did allow wars of intervention. The legitimacy of this intervention rested on the premise that only one party in a war could have justice on its side. To intervene on the side of justice was not an act of aggression, although to intervene on the side of injustice would be so. He allowed for conscientious objection for Christians who might have religious scruples. He denounced the idea of a professional military in preference for a civilian army mustered for the occasion. Still he accepted military necessity so that he proposed few limits to what soldiers could properly do.

This rule that only proper authority could declare war was reiterated by Samuel Rachel (1628-1691);[31] Johann Textor (1638-1701);[32] Samuel Pufendorf (1632-1694);[33] and Emmerich Vattel (1714-1767).[34] However, by the eighteenth century, in part coincident with the rise of democratic aspirations, Christian Wolff (1679-1754) urged a reformulation of the locus of authority. He commented:

> The ruler of the state is bound at least to seek the consent either of the people or of the nobles. But in a democracy or a popular state since the sovereignty rests with the entire people, the right of war also rests with the people.[35]

In 1836 Henry Wheaton in his *Elements of International Law* believed that he summed up the conclusions of the preceding centuries:

> The right of making war, as well as of authorizing reprisals or other acts of vindictive retaliation, belongs in every civilized nation, to the supreme power of the State.[36]

By the nineteenth century the requirement that wars be properly declared was divorced from any notions of justice. Wars were legal once they were announced. Indeed, by this time even the declaration was no longer essential.

JUST REASONS FOR DECLARING WAR

The views differed markedly among the various jurists. Victoria had denied that the aim of spreading one religion or of suppressing another was a legitimate aim of war. In his general summation of proper ends Victoria had remarked that there was "a single and only just cause for commencing war, namely a wrong received."[37] The nature of such a wrong was not, however, specified. Belli had stated that a just cause was required, but his list of acceptable causes was less than discriminating, and included the following:

altars, home fires, for children and wives...from the desire to
escape injury or even to avenge the same, whether a person
is righting a wrong done to himself, or to some other, his
ally, friend, or associate.[38]

Wrongs of such generality fail to distinguish the wars of one nation
from another. They all have altars, wives, etc. His further remark that
wars may be justly waged in "defense of liberty and fatherland"[39] meant
that no reason really needed to be given. Ayala's list of just reasons
included defense of empire, protection of friends and allies, and taking
vengeance for a wrong received.[40] Alberico Gentili seemed to doubt
that an unjust war was possible even in principle, since "even a war of
vengeance and an offensive war may be waged justly."[41] Suarez restated
the Augustinian three criteria but allowed wars in response to,

seizure by a prince of another's property ...denial without
reasonable cause of the common rights of nations, such as
the right of transit over highways, trading in common...and
grave injury to one's reputation or honour.[42]

Grotius believed that the authorities agreed upon three undisputed and
justifiable reasons for going to war: defense, the recovery of property,
and punishment.[43] We are left with little guidance in all of this, and in
the absence of any adjudicating judge, nations were left on their own
in justifying their reasons of state.

ARE THERE UNJUST REASONS FOR WAGING WAR?

In spite of the vagueness with which the subject of just causes
was presented, most of the writers nevertheless felt keenly that unjust
reasons existed. The oldest and simplest answer was that given by
Victoria which proscribed wars over religious difference. Ayala had
agreed with Victoria and had affirmed that not even the Pope or the
Roman Emperor could justify a war against infidels merely because
they were not Christian. Gentili repeated this claim, although he
doubted that the principle had much support in fact.[44] Suarez agreed
with this proscription against religious wars. [45] Unfortunately, the clerics
at Toledo had already decreed that heretics should be punished by war.
It should be asked whether wars over differences in political ideology
are also proscribed, a matter of contemporary relevance in view of the
American administration claims that the Soviet Union, for example, was
an "evil empire."
        Grotius did list as unacceptable reasons for going to war: fear of
a neighbor, the desire for richer land owned by another, the desire to

rule over others for their own good, though against their wills, and the claim to be the self-appointed leader of the world.[46] In view of the universal drives toward national expansion, Rachel had concluded that most wars of the past had been unjust and "not far removed from robbery."[47] Textor stated that not even the excuse of self-defense was adequate if one's own nation had caused the initial wrong.[48] In his list of unjust causes Pufendorf listed avarice, ambition, the desire for more and better lands, and the fear of neighbors. Preemptive wars were not justifiable, "unless it is established with moral and evident certitude that there is an intent to injure us."[49] In a world of suspicious nations such intent would normally be suspected.

By the eighteenth century little progress had been made in distinguishing just from unjust causes of war. Nations were presumed to have the right to go to war in their own perceived defense, so that issues of justice were irrelevant. Indeed, Vattel doubted that nations ever needed to refrain from declaring war.[50]

CAN JUSTICE BE ON BOTH SIDES?

Victoria answered this question with reservations. If justice were on both sides of the same war, and this was not precluded, it seemed to follow that the war would then be unjust for both sides. This was on the grounds that it was unjust to war against a nation which had justice on its side. In such cases Victoria allowed ignorance as an excuse.

> Assuming a demonstrable ignorance either of fact or law, it may be that on the side where true justice is the war is just in itself, while on the other side the war is just in the sense of being excused from sin by reason of good faith, because invincible ignorance is a complete excuse.[51]

Ayala denied such a claim could have any sense.[52] Gentili said that the entire question was irrelevant, since the answer was an obvious affirmative.[53] Zouche agreed with Victoria and remarked that "two persons may go to war justly, that is in good faith on each side."[54] Vattel spoke for the majority when he concluded that wars "must be regarded as equally lawful."[55]

MAY CITIZENS REFUSE TO FIGHT?

Practice and principle were in such conflict that the jurists were prompted simply to report the differences without passing any judgments. The question was complicated by the presence of conflicting premises. On the one hand, kings were empowered to issue a call to arms of their subjects, while at the same time the conscientious subjects were thought to deserve some recourse to refuse to go to war for scurrilous kings. Most writers accepted both concerns. If the king was justified in his call to arms, then citizens would be wrong to refuse the call. This was not a matter of conscientious objection to war in principle, since to grant that would open the door to a right of revolution.

Victoria was typical of most writers on this matter. He argued that if the subject was convinced of the injustice of the war, then he ought not to serve in it, even at the command of his prince.[56] At the same time Victoria admitted that princes were not obligated to give their citizens reasons for every war. Indeed, if subjects were obligated only when their conscience permitted, the state might never get an army for its legitimate defense. He added,

> If subjects in case of doubt do not follow their prince to the war, they expose themselves to the risk of betraying their State to the enemy, and this is a much more serious thing than fighting against an enemy despite doubt.[57]

The moral here is unclear. On his part the citizen may express his conscientious scruples, while the prince on his part has the right to command the citizens for military service. As between the two rights, that of the prince was obviously the more important.

Belli was also undecided whether the citizen had a right to refuse the call of the prince to arms. He cited the dictum of St. Augustine to the effect that citizens were obligated to obey even clearly wicked rulers. At the same time, he cited certain proconsuls who had claimed that if the injustice of the prince was,

> clear and manifest, the vassal was not bound....If, however, the injustice of the lord is not established...obedience must be rendered.[58]

Grotius commented on the difficulty of reconciling citizen conscience with princely demands. In those cases where the citizen was dissatisfied with the explanations of the prince as to the reasons for the war, Grotius suggested that such citizens be given extraordinary taxes as an alternative to military service. This would also serve as a test of the seriousness of the conscience of the objector. Since there was never a lack of willing recruits, there was no pressing reason why the prince should exacerbate what could become a touchy domestic situation. Indeed, as late as the American Civil War monetary substitutes were fairly common in the case of unwilling recruits.[59] In the case of Christians Grotius was even more lenient. He remarked,

> It does not seem right that Christians should be compelled to serve against their will; the reason is that to refrain from military service, even when it is permissible to serve, is the mark of a somewhat greater holiness.[60]

His attitude was not typical and may have reflected that Holland was the refuge for many dissident Protestant movements. The distinguished Jacobus Arminius (1560-1609) had already challenged the military ideals of the day, and he was Grotius's professor at the University of Leyden. The latitude allowed by Grotius was rejected by Vattel who insisted that citizens were obligated to serve when the prince gave a call to arms.[61]

Where do we now stand as a result of these writers? Is there a proper just war notion? Did they support the notion of just reasons for declaring war? The conclusion seems to be that kings have the right to declare war and that they have the right to command their citizens to fight in such a war. In the absence of any body, clerical or legal, to make the determination as to whether a war was needlessly aggressive, we had to accept the right of nations to declare war. Just war doctrine at this point played no serious role. It proved either incapable or unwilling to require surrender on the part of a prince. This aspect of just war theory was laid to rest by the time of Grotius. It still remains germane, however, to ask what role just war theory could play in assessing the means of war.

NOTES

1.   Aristotle, *Politics* (New York: Random House, 1943), Ch. VIII, 1256.

2.   Cicero, *Offices* (London: Lackington, 1820), pp. 25-27.

3.   Augustine, *The City of God*, Bk. I, paragraph 7.

4.   Augustine's reasoning on these matters may be followed in his *Reply to Faustus the Manichaean*, Bk. XXII, paragraph 70; *Questions Concerning the Heptateuch*, No. 10; *Letter CXXXVIII*, paragraph 15; and *The City of God*, Bk. XIX, Section 7.

5.   Augustine, *The City of God*, Bk. XIX, paragraph 12.

6.   Oliver Thatcher and Edgar H. McNeal, *A Sourcebook for Medieval History* (New York: Charles Scribner's, 1907), p. 412.

7.   *Ibid.*, p. 403.

8.   Leon Gautier, *Chivalry* (New York: Routledge and Sons, 1891), p. 9.

9.   *The Statesman's Book of John of Salisbury*, (tr.) John Dickenson (New York: Russell and Russell, 1963), p. 198.

10.   *Ibid.*, p. 199.

11.   *Ibid.*, p. 201.

12.   *Ibid.*, p. 213.

13.   *Ibid.*, pp. 211-212.

14.   Cited in Maurice Hugh Keen, *The Laws of War in the Late Middle Ages* (London: Routledge and Kegan Paul, 1965), pp. 64-65.

15.   St. Thomas Aquinas, *Summa Theologica*, Question XL.

16.   *Ibid.*, Reply to Objection Four.

17.   *Ibid.*, Article One.

18.   *Ibid.*, Reply to Question Two.

19. St. Thomas Aquinas, *Questions Concerning the Heptateuch*, Question I.

20. St. Thomas Aquinas, *Summa Theologica*, Question XL, Fourth Article.

21. *Ibid.*, Ch. 15.

22. Giovanni da Legnano, *The Law of War* (Oxford: Oxford University Press, 1919), Ch. 12.

23. Cf. Joseph McKenna, "Ethics and War: A Catholic View," *American Political Science Review* (September, 1960), pp. 647-658.

24. Franciscus de Victoria, *On the Indians* (Washington: Carnegie Foundation, 1917), Question 2, paragraph 422.

25. *Ibid.*, Question 2, paragraph 427.

26. Pierino Belli, *A Treatise on Military Matters* (Oxford: Clarendon, 1936), Ch. V.3.

27. Francisco Suarez, *The Three Theological Virtues* (Oxford: Clarendon, 1944), Disputation XIII, Section 2, paragraph 1.

28. *Ibid.*, paragraph 6.

29. Hugo Grotius, *On the Law of War and Peace* (Oxford: Clarendon, 1944), Bk. III, Ch. 3, Section 4.

30. *Ibid.*, Bk. IV, Ch. 1, Sections 1, 3.

31. Samuel Rachel, *The Law of Nature and of Nations* (Washington: Carnegie Foundation, 1916), Section XLIV.

32. Johann Textor, *Synopsis of the Law of Nations* (Washington: Carnegie Foundation, 1916), Ch. XVII, paragraph 49.

33. Samuel Pufendorf, *The Duties of Men and Citizens According to Natural Law* (New York: Oxford University Press, 1927), Ch. XVI, Section 8.

34. Emmerich Vattel, *The Law of Nations* (Washington: Carnegie Foundation, 1916), Ch. 1, paragraph 4.

35. Christian Wolff, *The Law of Nations* (Oxford: Clarendon, 1934), paragraph 614.

36. Henry Wheaton, *Elements of International Law*. (Oxford: Clarendon, 1936), Pt. II, Ch.I, paragraph 294.

37. Victoria, *On the Indians*, paragraph 13.

38. Belli, *Treatise*, paragraph 9.

39. *Ibid.*, paragraph 13.

40. Balthazar Ayala, *Three Books on the Law of War and on the Duties Connected with War and Military Discipline* (Washington: Carnegie Foundation, 1912), Ch. II. Questions 11, 12, and 13.

41. Alberico Gentili, *On the Law of War* (Oxford: Clarendon, 1933), paragraphs 61, 62.

42. Suarez, *The Theological Virtues*, Disputation XIII, Section 1, paragraph 7.

43. Grotius, *The Law of War*, Bk. II, Ch. XII.

44. Gentili, *On the Law of War*, Ch. X, paragraph 71.

45. Suarez, *The Theological Virtues*, Disputation XIII, Section 5, paragraphs 1-5.

46. Grotius, *The Law Of War*, Bk. II, Ch. XII, Sections V, VII, XI, XII, and XIII.

47. Rachel, *The Law of Nature*, Section XXXIX.

48. Textor, *Synopsis*, Ch. XVII, Question 47.

49. Pufendorf, *The Duties*, Bk. VIII, paragraph 5.

50. Vattel, *The Law*, Ch. III, paragraph 27.

51. Victoria, *On the Indians*, paragraph 32.

52. Ayala, *The Law*, Ch. II, paragraph 34.

53. Gentili, *The Law*, Bk. I, Ch. VI, paragraphs 48, 49, 51.

54. Richard Zouche, *An Exposition of Fecial Law and Procedure, or the Law Between Nations and Questions Concerning the Same* (Washington: Carnegie Foundation, 1911), Section VI.2.

55. Vattel, *The Law*, Ch. III, paragraph 39.

56. Victoria, *On the Indians*, paragraph 30.

57. *Ibid.*, paragraph 31.

58. Belli, *Treatise*, Ch. II, paragraphs 1 and 3.

59. Grotius, *The Law of War*, Bk. II, Ch. XXVI, Section 5.

60. *Ibid.*, Section 5.

61. Vattel, *The Law*, Ch. II, paragraph 8.

Chapter 3
THEORIES
OF THE MEDIEVAL JURISTS

Just war theory was unable to provide guidance in the matter of the declaration of war, especially as such declaration required a just cause. The sovereignty of nations coupled with the military obligation to fight to victory in war made concern with the justice of the ends irrelevant. Waging war was a national right, and every nation had the same right. While, in principle, just war theory entailed that some nations did not deserve to survive and that surrender might be the only just option, in fact such conclusions were not drawn. To do so would have undermined the principle of sovereign nationalism. It was possible, however, to apply just war criteria to the matter of the means of war. In a world where wars were legal, rules could exist for how wars were to be justly waged. One of the criteria of both Augustine and Aquinas concerned the justice of the intentions. It was this concern from which proportionality was derived. Even in a world where the ends were taken for granted, it was possible to assess the means by which nations sought to achieve those ends. When the jurists faced these matters, they had inherited along with the just war criteria, the doctrines of military necessity, the right of armies to use reprisal, and the obligation of soldiers to obey superior orders. As we shall see, the military criteria and the just war criteria were in conflict.

WERE THERE LIMITS TO PROPORTIONALITY?

Victoria had raised this matter at the time of the Spanish war against the American Indians. He had asked, "What kind of stress is lawful in a just war?"[1] His answer was that everything which the defense of the commonwealth required was lawful. The prince could order whatever was militarily necessary. Yet, even this permission was not without exception. For example, he stated,

> If some one city cannot be recaptured without greater evils befalling the State, such as the devastation of many cities,

great slaughter of human beings... it is indubitable that the
Prince is bound rather to give up his own rights and abstain
from war.[2]

Clearly what was needed was a prince who could calculate with some
Aristotelian sense of proportion, or some objective yardstick and some
objective agency to use this yardstick to calculate what those "greater
evils" were. How was Victoria to persuade his prince when it was
"indubitable" that he should abstain from some strategy? How would
the prince know that the means he was considering exceeded the worth
of the ends he was pursuing? The fact was that the Spanish prince did
not have Victoria's interest in the issue at all nor did he take his
advice.

Suarez was convinced that it would be unreasonable to inflict
grave harm when the injustice was slight.[3] However, Suarez had no
criteria for making this determination, nor could he calculate when the
permissible bounds had been passed. When, for example, would a
reprisal cause too much harm? Or was the right of reprisal so
important that any war act was allowed? The earliest efforts to identify
proportionality emphasized that the killing of women, children, old
persons, and the clergy was not justifiable. Grotius had added to the
list of protected persons merchants, farmers, and prisoners of war.[4] In
actual practice, however, as Rachel pointed out, nations drew no such
lines at all. Armies assumed that they had license which allowed, "The
killing of women and children, and the slaughter, at any time, of
prisoners and those who wish to surrender."[5] Positive practice sanctioned, in addition, the use of plunder and poison, if the failure to use
them exposed a nation to some military disadvantage. Customs on these
matters differed as did the views of the jurists. Textor rejected the plea
of military necessity as a justification for abhorrent acts. He insisted
that "some arithmetical proportion should exist between the hurt... and
the warlike licence allowed."[6] The proportion, however, remained
elusive, and anarchy in the application was the rule. The remarks of
Pufendorf illustrated the general lack of any rule, when he granted to
each nation the right to make its own calculations.

If a man feels that the avenging of an injury done him will
mean more evil than good, he acts in a just and praiseworthy
manner in refusing to punish it in recourse to war.[7]

Understandably not every prince or soldier made the same
calculations. Proportionality was not a very precise notion, despite the
general belief that some acts were excessive. In fact, nations usually
judged their opponents to be acting in excess while insisting that their

own acts were in moderation. Pufendorf had allowed nations "a licence to use force against him in any degree or so far as I think desirable."[8] Bynkerschoek concluded, "In my opinion every force is lawful in war....Does it matter what means we use to accomplish it?"[9] Wolff hoped that nations would use force moderately while still allowing them to use whatever force seemed required.[10] While deploring acts which were "essentially evil and unlawful", Vattel still permitted princes to use whatever force was required to subdue an enemy.[11] Were there no absolute limits? Could total devastation be allowed? Vattel's remarks showed that no limits seemed to exist:

> A sovereign has the right to do to an enemy whatever is necessary to weaken him and disable him from maintaining an unjust position.[12]

Discussion of proportion without any measuring device did not inspire confidence that monarchs would ever set self-imposed limits to their war making where defeat was a possibility. As long as military necessity was determined by military strategists, rather than by moral theorists, proportion could never serve as a criterion. Proportionality would remain mere prudence in the conservation of military resources. The military leader might be well advised to conserve firepower where a shortage of ammunition occurred, but if arms were abundant, there was no further reason to be conservative. Measuring scales did not exist, so that advice about limits made little sense. Proportionality was a private assessment in the absence of any supranational standard. By 1863, Wheaton, while supporting the milder views of Grotius and Vattel, and deploring the excesses of Bynkerschoek and Wolff, had to admit that, "The law of nature has not precisely determined how far an individual is allowed to make use of force."[13]

The situation was one where proportion was urged but no way existed to interpret what proportion could possibly mean. In spite of this, subsequent peace congresses and the various military manuals still spoke of proportionality as desirable and meaningful. Indeed, the Nuremberg and Tokyo Trials appealed to the notion in sentencing soldiers for having committed excesses.

MAY ALL SOLDIERS BE SLAIN?

In the medieval period, through the display of varied colored flags or pennons, and the issuance of certain threats or requests for surrender, rules were created to help control the proper occasion for killing the enemy and the numbers killed. For example, in wars of "no quarter" the total population could be annihilated. The refusal of a town to surrender exposed it to the right of the opponent to kill every resident in it. Victoria raised the question, "Whether in a just war it is lawful to kill, at any rate, all of the guilty."[14] His answer was that in war, and in the heat of battle, everyone who resists may be slain. May we continue to slay the enemy after he has surrendered? In the case of war against unbelievers, Victoria thought that it would be expedient to kill everyone. In the case of wars against Christians, however,

> I think that they may not be killed, not only not all of them,
> but not even one of them, if the presumption is that they
> entered the strife in good faith.[15]

The implication was that if good faith was not evident, then total slaughter would be permitted. The denial of good faith to unbelievers robbed the answer of that universality needed to make it the basis for a law of war. Once wars were fought for economic, political, social, let alone religious ideologies, the temptation would exist to treat all ideological opponents as lacking in good faith.

Grotius extended the right to kill the enemy after surrender, not simply the soldiers who had born arms, or leaders who had stirred the nation to war, but everyone who resided in the enemy territory. Even prisoners of war lacked protection.[16] Textor moderated this position. He accepted the thesis that every armed enemy may be slain in battle, or even afterward if they were in a position to harm us, but he denied that nations had any right to kill soldiers who had laid down their arms. He urged, further, that distinctions be drawn between those who had actively promoted the war and willingly entered the army, from those who had entered under duress. These latter "can more easily and readily be spared than the former."[17] Wolff also counselled moderation and remarked,

> Since one ceases to be an enemy as soon as he is in my
> power... it is not allowable to kill those who have surrendered
> unconditionally.[18]

While Vattel supported Wolff in this matter, exceptions were made in the case of those enemies who had committed grave breaches of the laws of war. In such cases reprisals in kind were permitted.[19]

Since it was obviously in the best interests of soldiers to be given some protection when they became *hors de combat*, general support has existed for the obligation of belligerents to take prisoners and to protect them for the duration of a war. This was the position of the first U.S. Army manual, *General Orders 100*. It was also the position of the judges at Nuremberg and Tokyo.

ARE ANY EXEMPT FROM BEING CASUALTIES?

Historically, old men, women, and children were in a class of supposedly absolutely protected persons. If, in fact, this protection was not always honored, still, in principle, lip service was paid to it. Victoria had claimed that even in wars against the Turks it was not allowed to kill women and children.[20] At the same time he added that it would not be permitted to kill foreigners, clerics, guests, or members of religious orders. However, practice did not accord with this, and Belli was moved to note that the principle was little observed.[21] While Grotius approved of the protection of women and children, he noted that it was common practice to kill even these, and that the laws of war even sanctioned it.[22] Nonetheless, he considered it to be a sign of commendable mercy to spare women and children "except for reasons that are weighty."[23] The permission to kill them under "weighty" reasons left the status of the original prohibition unclear. Since the judgment of "weightiness" was made by the litigants, this could scarcely qualify as a law of war.

In cases where women had been soldiers the same punishment as for men was warranted. Zouche said that where this was the case, then they were not, in the appropriate sense, women at all.[24] While Wolff thought that it was not proper to kill those weakened by age, disease, or mental incapacity, he still maintained that in war every citizen of the enemy country was an enemy. Vattel stated that even though women and children were enemies in the sense of total war, they still ought not to be killed. Indeed, he claimed that this was so generally believed that,

> If occasionally an enraged or unrestrained soldier goes so far as to outrage female virtue, or to massacre women, children, and old men, the officers regret such excesses and endeavor to check them, and a wise and humane general even punishes the offenders when he can.[25]

Soldiers in the field will rarely be capable of understanding the meaning of these juristic qualifications. If the occasions when women and children were slain were as common as Belli and Grotius claimed, then it would be additionally difficult to explain in what sense and under what conditions laws existed to protect them. In any event, it appeared to be either military necessity or simply the inhumanity of the commander which tolerated this kind of killing. Once the premise of total war was accepted, and once every citizen became an enemy, then the old combatant-non-combatant distinction no longer existed. It was not sufficiently comforting to know that the humane officer would show regret and would, if possible, punish offenders. As long as the practice was widespread, and as long as it was militarily commendable, there was little chance that either regret or punishment would occur. In spite of this, the killing of everyone has tended to be deplored. This seemed to be the case in the American public reaction to the events at Son My and My Lai in Vietnam, as well as to what had occurred in extermination camps under the Germans. The judgments at Nuremberg were not sufficiently clear on the matter of whether women, children, and old men could ever be killed under the guise of military necessity. Aerial bombardment guaranteed that innocent civilians would be slain, yet the judges did not prosecute the German air forces. Was this due to the fact that to object to the killing of civilians by the air forces was tantamount to advocating that aerial warfare be banned altogether? Were they not prepared to do this? However, if land troops were commanded to cease operating extermination camps this did not mean that the army would cease to function. Did the Nuremberg judges excuse the killing of the innocent from the air because it was militarily impossible to avoid it, while they condemned the extermination camps because they were militarily avoidable hence not necessary?

The taking of hostages had been an accepted part of military strategy. This was particularly practical when the hostages were wealthy or famous. In either case, hostage taking put pressure on an opponent. But was it proper to kill hostages? Ordinarily it was assumed that hostages were like soldiers *hors de combat*, hence, innocent, so that killing them would be prohibited. Unfortunately, the threat to kill hostages who were women, children, and religious or political leaders was commonly militarily effective. If the threat to kill them was an idle one, then the entire process of taking hostages would lose its effectiveness. Victoria had said that hostages could be sold into slavery but they ought not to be killed.[26] Zouche said that hostages who attempted to run away should not be killed for having tried, but they could be killed during the attempt.[27] By the nineteenth century the taking and slaying of hostages had become common military custom.

FORBIDDEN STRATEGIES AND WEAPONS

The answers of the jurists were conditioned, as we might expect, by the doctrine of military necessity on the one hand and the right of reprisal on the other. In the case of reprisal an army against whom a forbidden act had been done could legitimately do the forbidden act in return. Otherwise forbidden acts committed in reprisal were not against the rules or laws of war. Victoria had noted that if to storm a city where many innocent civilians lived would have little effect on the outcome of the war, then such storming ought not to be done. On the other hand, if it served a helpful strategic role, such strategy was permitted. Thus Victoria seemed to be saying that certain strategies ought not to be undertaken unless they served a useful military function. Military necessity removed an otherwise forbidden strategy from the forbidden list. He noted that under necessity,

> It is certainly lawful to despoil the innocent of goods and things which the enemy would use against us... nay, it is lawful to take the money of innocent and to burn and destroy their grain and kill their horses, if this is requisite in order to sap the enemy's strength.[28]

Ayala considered such losses by the civilians to be normal consequences of war. This matter will reappear in all the versions of the American Army manuals as a prohibition against the bombing of unfortified cities. At the time of the Nuremberg and Tokyo Trials aerial bombing of civilian centers was such standard practice by the air forces of all armies that no German or Japanese was ever prosecuted for the deliberate aerial attack on civilians. The Allied bombing of Dresden, Berlin, and Tokyo, not to forget their atomic bombing of Hiroshima and Nagasaki, meant that a *tu quoque* protest would have been made by the lawyers for the Axis accused had the Allies decided to prosecute them for making deliberate war on civilians from the air. That the Allies did prosecute the Axis soldiers for deliberate war on civilians in extermination camps implied, in part, that such killings served no useful military end and were furthermore avoidable. Did the Allies also believe that the latter deeds were more inhumane than doing similar acts from the air?

Prohibitions against the use of poison originated in ancient times. Church councils forbade such use. Part of the reason for the continued antipathy to the use of poison was because it was invisible and, hence, not sporting. In addition, it was not discriminating and killed civilians as likely as soldiers. That no practical defense existed against poison may have influenced armies, in their own defense, to agree to ban such a weapon. Poisoning the water supply was generally indicted, although it was permissible to pollute water by more visible means such as throwing a dead carcass in the well. Zouche remarked that when the Spanish had been besieged by the French at Naples, the Spanish had poisoned the French water supply, an act which Zouche condemned.[29] He also condemned the act of the Italians who sent infected prostitutes into the French military camps. Rachel claimed that civilized nations did not use poison, either in their missiles or against the enemy's water supply.[30] Pufendorf said that civilized nations drew the line at the use of poison, assassination, and the taking of bribes.[31]

Pufendorf asserted that while it was proper to deceive the enemy, acts of perfidy were not to be tolerated.

> One may still use craft or deceit against an enemy provided that this does not entail perfidy and the violation of pacts and pledged faith.[32]

He illustrated the difference between an ordinary act of deception in which one pretends to have more arms or troops than he really possesses, or pretends to attack in one direction while intending to attack in another from perfidy. Perfidy, on the contrary, might consist of wearing the uniform of the enemy, raising a flag of surrender when one has no intention of doing so, or shooting emissaries who carry the flag of truce. Bynkerschoek, who had claimed "everything is legitimate against an enemy"[33] gave only this one exception. Perfidy gave an unfair advantage to weak nations over strong ones, who, after all, deserved to be the winners. Furthermore, the practice of perfidy undermined useful military strategies.

On only two issues was there much agreement: the use of poison and the practice of perfidy. Vattel scorned those writers who claimed that the manner of killing was of no importance. He classified treacheries by degrees. Poison, for example, was more revolting than assassination. Poisoned weapons were, however, less objectionable than poisoning the water supply.[34] In the nineteenth century Wheaton summed up the matter when he affirmed that if nations could not achieve their ends by any other means, they could resort to measures normally forbidden.[35]

MUST THERE BE A DECLARATION OF WAR?

The medieval claim was that wars had to be declared by the duly constituted authority. In part, the declaration signalled that if any laws of war existed, they would now take effect. But suppose that surprise would be a military advantage. Must the king or prince still make a public declaration in advance of his intentions to attack?

Belli believed that the intent of the rule was to allow a reasonable delay between the announcement and the attack. Thus a hasty or ill-conceived war might be avoided by the required delay. He insisted that no attack should be made prior to this announcement. To do otherwise was to be treacherous.[36] Grotius insisted upon a public declaration even though neither political nor military custom supported him.[37] Indeed, Zouche noted instances in which the declaration had been dispensed with entirely, namely in defensive wars, those against known enemies, and wars against rebels and deserters.[38] Textor observed, "these solemnities in declaring war have fallen into desuetude in modern time."[39] Still he insisted that the declaration ought to be made. At least the neighboring nations needed to know when a state of war existed. Yet, the practice of ignoring the declaration prompted Pufendorf to distinguish between declared and undeclared wars, while claiming that each was a proper kind of war.[40] Bynkerschoek dismissed the requirement as, "Not demanded by an exigency of reason, that while it is a thing which may properly be done, it cannot be required as a matter of right."[41] Wolff said that, of course, defensive wars needed no declaration, and even in offensive wars, the declaration could be omitted if the enemy did not admit envoys.[42] Only Vattel held fast in his counsel of perfection that no one was excused from declaring war simply because his neighbor had not done so.[43]

By the nineteenth century each nation had its own criteria to determine who may properly declare war, while at the same time the requirement that it had to be declared at all seemed to have disappeared. Legal advantages appeared to exist for a declaration, such as signalling that, if there were laws of war, they would now apply. This was still the customary interpretation at the time of the Nuremberg and Tokyo Trials, and as a consequence none of the accused were prosecuted solely for offenses prior to the official outbreak of the war. Where surprise was a military advantage, strategic reasons supported the army preference to attack and let the declaration follow. In the special cases of Vietnam, and the invasions of Grenada or Nicaragua United States troops could be sent into battle by a simple presidential decree, bypassing Congress, as long as no one called it a war. If laws of war existed, then as in the cases of Vietnam or Nicaragua, did this mean that laws did not apply, since no war had been declared? The notion of war crimes presupposes a war, and the declaration of war was the clearest evidence that a war was taking place.

Wheaton noted in 1836 that the practice of declaring war had virtually ceased by the seventeenth century. Present usage, he noted, was to make a declaration only when it was useful,

> To distinguish in a treaty of peace those acts which are to
> be accounted lawful effects of war, from those which either
> nation may consider as naked wrongs, and for which they
> may, under certain circumstances, claim reparation.[44]

Beyond this prudential consideration no further legal, military, or moral reasons appeared for letting an enemy know in advance that an attack was imminent. Indeed, in the United States, the lack of any such announcement served the advantage of keeping the fact of attack from the American people and even the Congress. This had been particularly so in the forays led by the CIA, or the Department of Defense, or the many attacks led by the Delta Force, created in 1979 as a secret counterterrorism unit designed to bypass Congressional limitations against such vigilante actions. Between 1770 and 1870 there were at least eighty occasions in Europe alone where wars were waged without any declaration.[45]

MUST SUPERIOR ORDERS BE OBEYED?

The earliest military writings presumed that, as a matter of course, superior orders were to be obeyed. It was not until 1944 that the American Army manual, *The Rules of Land Warfare,* was revised in such a way that the appeal to superior orders was no longer an automatic excuse for what soldiers did in war. Soldiers in the past had not been expected to evaluate the orders they received, nor were they exposed to possible prosecution for obeying them.

Suarez stated that generals were under no obligation to worry about the propriety of the orders they gave and that soldiers who followed those orders were exempt from legal or moral blame for doing so. Soldiers were the mere instruments of their prince.[46] Although Belli had affirmed that soldiers ought not to obey unjust orders, he also noted that soldiers were rarely in any position to evaluate those orders. He cited with approval the dictum of Augustine that unquestioning obedience was the soldier's duty. "Obedience must be rendered when the latter calls."[47] Ayala recommended that in a monarchic state the soldier was well advised to follow authority.[48] By the time of Vattel this obedience was beyond dispute.

> Subordinate officers, in making agreements, bind those who are subject to their control, with respect to all matters concerning which they have the power and the right to give commands.[49]

But where in all of this can we find evidence that the superior orders were bound by some limits? We are advised that soldiers must obey, but we are not enlightened as to whether those who gave the orders needed to take care that they did not give inhumane orders. For several reasons these international jurists were unable to provide any firm evidence of recognized laws or rules of war. In the first place, the demise of just war theory as it applied to the ends for which wars were fought meant, in effect, that the means were left without a sense of proportionality. Just war theory entailed that unjust wars ought not to be fought at all. But if wars were a sovereign right of nations, then there were no unjust wars. Furthermore, just war theory insisted upon some moderation in means. But if war was a right, then winning the war was also a right. If winning was a right, then how could laws prevent a nation from using any useful strategy or weapon for waging the war to victory?

In the second place, the doctrine of military necessity supported and conditioned this right. If every law of war was conditioned by military necessity, then the only laws left would be those forbidding what armies did not intend to do in any event. Laws of war presupposed limits, while national sovereignty presupposed no limits which curtailed the exercise in war of whatever was required to win. Nations could always do whatever their perceived security required. Surrender, while a theoretical obligation in just war doctrine, was inconceivable to military necessity. Armies might stand judged for having done some inhumane act when it was not militarily necessary, but in the absence of an international judge to determine what was militarily necessary, each army commander made the judgment for himself. This meant that the Nuremberg judges might rule that the extermination camps were not militarily necessary, but did the judges have precedent for claiming that such camps were wrong because they were inhumane? Furthermore, if orders needed to be obeyed, who was going to identify when improper orders had been given? Just war theory would judge a wrong order on grounds that it was inhumane and excessive, not simply on the grounds that it was not militarily needed to win the war. Thus, these jurists might insist that rules existed but they had little evidence from custom for identifying what these rules might be. Generals might deplore the actions of brutal troops as unchivalrous, but this was not a law of war which could assist the judges at Nuremberg. The offenses named at Nuremberg were not the actions of renegade or disobedient soldiers. They were the simple acts of soldiers doing what was conventional custom for soldiers. This, as we shall consider, was also a question in the trials of those prosecuted for the events at Son My and My Lai. Were the actions of Calley, Schwartz, and Hutto standard army procedure, or were they the acts of renegade and exceptional soldiers? To answer such a question requires that we determine whether there are limits beyond which the appeal to military necessity cannot be made.

NOTES

1. Franciscus de Victoria, *On the Indians* (Washington: Carnegie Foundation, 1917), Section III, paragraphs 15-18.

2. *Ibid.*

3. Francisco Suarez, *The Three Theological Virtues* (Oxford: Clarendon, 1944), Disputation XIII, Section IV, 804.

4. Hugo Grotius, *The Law of War and Peace* (Oxford: Clarendon, 1925), Bk. III, Ch. XI and XII.

5. Samuel Rachel, *Dissertations on The Law of Nature and of Nations* (Washington: Carnegie Foundation, 1916), XLVI and XLVII.

6. Johann Wolfgang Textor, *Synopsis of the Law of Nations* (Washington: Carnegie Foundation, 1916), Ch. XVII, Section 3.

7. Samuel von Pufendorf, *The Law of Nature and of Nations* (Oxford, Clarendon, 1934), Bk. VIII, Ch. VI, Section 884.

8. *Ibid.*

9. Cornelius van Bynkerschoek, *Questions of Public Law* (Oxford: Clarendon, 1930), Ch. I, paragraph 3.

10. Christian Wolff, *The Law of Nations* (Oxford: Clarendon, 1934), paragraph 782.

11. Emmerich de Vattel, *The Law of Nations or the Principles of Natural Law* (Washington: Carnegie Foundation, 1916), Ch. VIII, paragraph 138.

12. *Ibid.*, paragraph 138.

13. Henry Wheaton, *Elements of International Law* (Oxford: Clarendon, 1936), P. IV, Ch. II, paragraph 342.

14. Victoria, *On the Indians*. Sections 44-48.

15. *Ibid.*

16. Grotius, *The Law of War*, Bk. III, Sections XII and XIV.

17. Textor, *Synopsis*. Ch. XVIII, paragraphs 17 and 19.

18. Wolff, *The Law*, paragraph 797.

19. Vattel, *The Law*. Ch. VIII, paragraphs 140-141.

20. Victoria, *On the Indians*, paragraph 37.

21. Pierino Belli, *A Treatise on Military Matters and Warfare* (Oxford: Clarendon, 1936), Ch. IX, Sections 1-7.

22. Grotius, *The Law of War*, Bk. III, Ch. IV. Section ix.

23. *Ibid.*, Bk. III, Ch. XI, Sections 8-9.

24. Richard Zouche, *An Exposition of Fecial Law and Procedure* (Washington: Carnegie Foundation, 1911), Section X, paragraphs 15-16.

25. Vattel, *The Law*, Ch. VIII, paragraph 145.

26. Victoria, *On the Indians*, paragraphs 453-454.

27. Zouche, *Exposition*, Section IX.

28. Victoria, *On the Indians*, Question 39, paragraph 451.

29. Zouche, *Exposition*, Section X, paragraph 5.

30. Rachel, *Dissertations*, paragraph XLVII.

31. Pufendorf, *The Duties*. Ch. XVI, paragraphs 6 and 12.

32. *Ibid.*, Bk. VIII, Ch. VI, paragraph 6.

33. Bynkerschoek, *Questions*, Bk. I, Ch. I,3.

34. Vattel, *The Law*, Ch. VIII, paragraph 155-156.

35. Wheaton, *Elements*, Pt. IV, paragraph 347.

36. Belli, *Treatise*, Pt. II, Ch. VIII, paragraphs 2-8.

37. Grotius, *The Law Of War*, Bk. III, Ch. III, paragraph 5.

38. Zouche, *Exposition*, Section X, paragraphs 1-2.

39. Textor, *Synopsis*, Ch. XVII, paragraphs 49-52.

40. Pufendorf, *The Law*, Ch. XVI, paragraph 7.

41. Bynkerschoek, *Questions*, Bk. I, Ch. II, paragraphs 6-9.

42. Wolff, *The Law*, paragraphs 710, 713, 714.

43. Vattel, *The Law*, Ch. IV, paragraph 59.

44. Wheaton, *Elements*, Pt. IV, paragraph 297.

45. George B. Davis, "The Amelioration of the Rules of War on Land," *The American Journal of International Law*, Vol. I (January, 1908), pp. 57-62.

46. Suarez, *The Theological Virtues*, Disputation XIII, paragraph 811.

47. Belli, *Treatise*, Ch. II, paragraphs 1-3.

48. Balthazar Ayala, *Three Books on the Law of War* (Washington: Carnegie Foundation, 1912), Ch. II, paragraphs 20, 21, 23.

49. Vattel, *The Law*, Ch. II, paragraph 23.

Chapter 4
RULES SET
BY INTERNATIONAL CONGRESSES

The international jurists were unable to provide evidence of any international conscience which went beyond mere military necessity. In 1864 at the first International Red Cross meetings at Geneva, we find the earliest attempt to provide this international conscience. The language and spirit of the Nuremberg and Tokyo indictments which the Nuremberg Charter enumerated presumed that the conventions which such congresses issued had some legal international status. The framers of the Nuremberg Charter were well aware that even if conviction that laws of war existed, the breaking of which would be crimes, these rules were conditioned by certain military and national commitments. Among these overriding commitments were the following:

o   War was a basic right of sovereign nations. It followed that no rule could ban war making in principle, where the hegemony of a nation was at stake.

o   Armies at war were guaranteed the right of reprisal and the appeal to military necessity whenever a resolution or rule might threaten military success. No commander expected rules to hinder him from pursuing a course to victory.

o   The commitment to sovereign nationalism precluded that any delegate to such an international congress could commit his nation to any rule overriding the nation's sovereignty.

o   Even where nations agreed to abide by some rules or prohibitions, the agreements could always be withdrawn under some conditions. In the case of The Hague declarations, for example, all commitments ceased to be binding in wars with non-signators.

In spite of these serious limitations, the conventions and resolutions of these congresses stood as symbolic testimony of a widespread desire to set some limits to the havoc which conventional war entailed.

THE GENEVA RED CROSS CONFERENCES

The first such congress was initiated by what came to be called the International Red Cross, August 22, 1864.[1] The occasion for the meeting was prompted by concern over the neglect of the sick and wounded at Solferino in the Franco-Austrian War of 1859. Henri Dunant was the prime mover, and the Swiss government was the convenor. The major result of the congress was a "Convention for the Amelioration of the Condition of the Wounded Armies in the Field." It established rudimentary rules for the protection of the sick and wounded soldiers through recognition of protections for doctors, nurses, and the ambulances and hospitals which aided them. It "entered into force" in 1865, although it was not until 1882 that the United States became a party. This delay was chiefly due to preoccupation with the Civil War. This meeting officially established the International Red Cross. Henri Dunant was awarded the first Nobel Peace prize in 1901 for his efforts. The United States was not a participant at that Congress. It should be noted that no limits were set as to what could be done to able-bodied soldiers in the process of wounding or killing them. They could be shot, stabbed, or clubbed until they were *hors de combat*. At that time the Conventions of the Congress applied to them.

The document had ten articles. Article I provided for the protection of the ambulance corps and hospitals as long as they functioned solely for medical purposes. Article II provided that the hospital staff, including drivers, nurses, doctors, superintendents, and chaplains all be given neutral status protection. Article V requested the same protection for the inhabitants of the enemy country who were assisting in medical care. The spirit of the Conventions was conciliatory and based on a sense of humanity. It was hoped that nations would endorse both the letter and the spirit of its Articles. No discussion of sanctions appeared either for compliance or punishment in case of infractions.

On October 20, 1868 a second Red Cross Congress was called.[2] It issued resolutions further elaborating the role of the medical staff and outlined procedures for quartering prisoners of war. It extended the same protections for the sick and wounded in sea casualties. Article VI, for example, provided that the passengers and crew of sinking ships be rescued, and that the ships which did this rescue be given neutral status until they had delivered their victims to a safe port. The United States was not a participant at this Conference either, although in 1882 the U.S. Congress approved both the 1864 and 1868 resolutions. In 1906 a revised Geneva "Convention for the Amelioration of the Condition of the Wounded in the Field" was issued. This attempted to incorporate the findings of The Hague Congress of 1899.

On July 17, 1929 a new Geneva Red Cross Conference was called to take account of events of World War I and the creation of newer weapons and strategies of warfare.[3] A "Convention on Treatment of Prisoners of War" endorsed The Hague Conventions of 1907 and added stipulations regarding the capture, evacuation, and imprisonment of war prisoners. Article II stated that prisoners should be treated humanely. Article VII stated that prisoners should not be needlessly exposed to dangers while being evacuated from the war zones. Article VIII stated that prisoners of war were not to be conventionally imprisoned at all unless their safety or health required it, nor should they be kept in climates for which their bodies were unaccustomed. Article XI required that the food for prisoners be on a par with what the troops of the captors had at their base camps. Article XCVI, however, allowed the High Contracting Parties to renounce the entire Convention. It stipulated further that the Convention would not take effect until one year after publication. The United States ratified the Convention on January 16, 1932, and it became part of the literature appealed to in both the U.S. Army manual, *Rules of Land Warfare*, and the principles of the Nuremberg Charter.

A draft of another Red Cross Congress was submitted in 1938 and placed on the agenda for meetings to be held in 1940. Due to World War II these meetings were postponed until 1949. In the interim the war crimes trials had been held following World War II. Since many of the offenses with which the Germans were charged had occurred prior to the military occupation, it became clear that the 1929 rules, which presupposed war, were inadequate. Attempts were made at the 1949 sessions to take care of these inadequacies. Four Conventions were issued at these 1949 Geneva sessions.[4]

- "**Convention for the Amelioration of the Wounded and Sick in Armed Forces in the Field.**" The 1929 Convention by that name had demanded only general respect for the protection of the wounded. The new Convention in Article XII listed specific acts required of the captors. Special mention was made that care be given regardless of race, sex, nationality, religion, or political persuasion. In addition to stating that prisoners ought not to be tortured, it affirmed that they were not to be used as guinea pigs in medical experiments.

o   "Convention for the Amelioration of the Condition of the
    Wounded, Sick, and Shipwrecked Members of the Armed
    Forces at Sea." This Convention contained sixty-seven
    articles which followed the *Rules Of Land Warfare*, and
    which granted to medical personnel at sea even greater
    protection than their counterparts on land.

o   "Convention Relative to the Treatment of Prisoners of
    War." The 1929 Convention had ninety-seven articles on
    this topic. The new Convention had one hundred forty-
    three articles. Article III contained the basic thrust of the
    entire Convention.

    Persons taking no active part in the hostilities inclu-
    ding members of the armed forces who have laid
    down their arms and those placed hors de combat by
    sickness, wounds, detention, or any other cause, shall
    in all circumstances be treated humanely.

    This was to be the case independently of race, religion,
    etc. The Article named the kinds of prohibited acts. These
    included murder, violence to life or person, mutilation,
    torture, outrages against dignity, and executions without
    trial. Article IV expanded the list of persons entitled to
    prisoner of war status to include members of resistance
    groups, civilian aircraft crews, newspaper correspondents,
    the merchant marine, and all inhabitants who spontaneously
    took up arms to resist the invading forces.

o   "Convention Relative to the Protection of Civilian Persons
    in Time of War." The first Geneva Convention of 1864
    had provided only for armed combatants, since it had been
    assumed that civilians would be spared the havoc of direct
    and intentional attack. The 1906 Convention did not
    anticipate the kinds of deeds which had become standard
    during World War I. What references it did make to
    civilians was to the preservation of family honor, life, and
    property.

An International Red Cross Conference of 1921 mentioned some
general principles concerning the mass deportation of civilians and the
taking of hostages. While a 1923 Red Cross Conference had called for
a meeting to deal specifically with civilian matters, the 1929 Conference
was still studying the question. In 1934 a draft was submitted for the

15th International Red Cross Conference in Tokyo but action was delayed until the 1940 meetings. Since these were not held, nations entered World War II without discussion of any of these Red Cross recommendations. There was no assurance, in any event from past Red Cross Conventions, that nations would have felt bound by them had they been in effect.

The 1949 Convention, therefore, in view of the mass deportations, mass exterminations, and widespread abuse of civilians which had occurred during the war, endeavored to speak to these offenses. A need was apparent to specify rules also for the protection of enemy aliens in belligerent territory, to protect sick and wounded who were civilians, to establish safe zones for them, and to provide for the internees of both occupied and unoccupied territories. Articles XXVII to XXXIV made provisions applicable to civilians wherever they might be. Articles XLVII and XLVIII dealt exclusively with occupied territory. They forbade the mass transportation of civilians and the forced labor of those under eighteen, and they decreed that only non-military labor should be required. It forbade labor without compensation. Article LV imposed the duty to provide adequate food and medical supplies to detainees. The Convention did not, however, offer these protections to citizens of any state which had renounced the Convention. The International Red Cross continues to meet and to propose limits. It remains the option, however, of nations to accept or to reject these Red Cross efforts.

THE HAGUE CONGRESSES

The rules of war appealed to by the Nuremberg judges, the breaking of which would be "war crimes," were based on the Conventions issued at the two Hague Congresses of 1899 and 1907.[5] Tsar Nicholas II of Russia called the first Congress in efforts to bring about an arms reduction and to discover more peaceful ways of settling international disputes. This first Congress included twenty-six nations. While they reached no unanimity on arms reductions, they did issue several Conventions and Declarations intended to outlaw certain war practices and weapons. There were three major Conventions dealing with war issues. The first was a "Convention for the Pacific Settlement of International Disputes." It expressed the hope that machinery would be developed for this end. The second "Convention with Respect to Laws and Customs of War on Land" contained sixty articles. Article IV required that prisoners of war be humanely treated. Article XXI affirmed that belligerents should respect the Geneva Convention of 1864 in their treatment of the sick and wounded. A third "Convention for the Adoption to Maritime Warfare the Principles of the Geneva Convention of 1864" contained twelve articles. The first five made specifications concerning the identification and protection of hospital ships. They were to be painted a distinctive white with a green band if they were military hospital ships, and with a red band if they were under the International Red Cross or some other private medical agency. Article VII urged that medical personnel be protected from attack or capture. Article VIII urged proper treatment of the sick or wounded. Article XI provided that all the Conventions would apply only in wars between nations which had signed agreement with the Conventions. They would not apply in wars where a non-signator was involved. These Conventions are commonly referred to in the literature as Hague I, II, and III.

In addition to these Conventions The Hague produced three relevant Declarations. The first was a "Declaration Prohibiting the Discharge of Projectiles from Balloons or by other Methods of a Similar Nature." The agreement was to remain in effect for a period of five years, and would be binding only in wars between signator nations. All nations in attendance, with the exception of Great Britain, were signators. The second "Declaration Prohibiting the Employment of Projectiles Containing Asphyxiating or Deleterious Gases" provided that the signators would refrain from using projectiles whose "sole" object was to diffuse such gases. It was implied that as long as projectiles had other functions, the use of gas would not be forbidden. Like the preceding, this was binding only in wars among signators. Neither Great Britain nor the United States was a signator. The third was a "Declaration Prohibiting the Employment of Bullets which Expand or Flatten Easily in the Human Body." These were called "dum dum" bullets named for a section in India where such bullets were used. Again the Declaration applied only in wars all the participants of which were signators. Neither Great Britain nor the United States was a signator. The limitation of the first Hague Congress was that its Conventions and Declarations had no sanction. A nation was excused simply by not signing, and in wars with non-signator nations, even those who had agreed not to commit the prohibited act were relieved of any obligation to live up to their commitment.

A second Hague Congress was called in 1907, again by Tsar Nicholas II, and with special encouragement from President Theodore Roosevelt. Forty-four governments were represented. Once again no agreement was reached on disarmament, although that had been a stated goal of the conference. Fifteen Declarations and Conventions were issued. The 1899 "Convention with Respect to the Laws and Customs of War" was reissued with minor changes. In Article XXIII, for example, the new Convention spoke of banning weapons which caused "unnecessary suffering," while the 1899 Convention had banned weapons which caused "superfluous injury." Article XXIV of the old Convention considered that ruses of war were "permissible," while the new Convention said that they were "allowable." In Article XXV of the old Convention it had been forbidden to attack unfortified cities, while the new Convention added the phrase "by whatever means." In Article XXVII of the old Convention "every care should be taken" to protect churches, hospitals, etc., while the new Convention dropped the word "every." The Convention concerning the dropping of projectiles from balloons was extended until a projected third Hague Congress, or until five years had passed. The Congress was never called and the nations entered World War I with this Convention expired. In any event it applied only in wars where all of the participant nations were signators.

There was a "Convention Concerning Bombardment by Naval Forces in Time of War." Article I forbade the bombing of unfortified cities, unless it was required by military exigency. Article II urged commanders to take steps to reduce "unnecessary suffering." The nature of such suffering was unspecified. There was a "Convention Relative to the Laying of Automatic Submarine Contact Mines." Recognizing that it would be impossible to outlaw the use of submarines, an attempt was made to reduce some its most undiscriminating aspects. Article I, for example, provided that all contact mines be so constructed that they became harmless once they had broken loose from their moorings. The same provision was proposed for torpedoes once they had missed their target. Article III required that the general areas where mines were laid be made known to the public so that peaceful shipping would not become victims. Submarines were unable to comply with the conventional rules requiring the attacking ship to pick up survivors. Either submarine warfare had to be banned altogether or else relieved of compliance with the rules for regular ships. Useful military weapons, however, are not abandoned for mere reasons of humanity, with the consequence that these recommendations were not adopted.

ST. PETERSBURG AND BRUSSELS CONGRESSES

In addition to these Hague and Geneva conferences other efforts were made to limit both weapons and strategies. In 1868, for example, upon invitation of the Imperial Cabinet of Russia, seventeen nations met at St. Petersburg to consider the desirability of forbidding the use of certain projectiles of war. This conference produced a "Declaration Renouncing The Use In War Of Certain Explosive Projectiles." In a brief thirty-eight line statement the Declaration affirmed that since the legitimate aim of states should be to weaken but not to annihilate the enemy forces, no weapon should be used which would uselessly aggravate the sufferings of the wounded. It was proposed that all projectiles weighing less than 400 grams, which were explosive or charged with flammable substances, be banned. The United States did not agree with this prohibition. In any event, it did not apply in wars with non-signators.

On August 27, 1874 a conference at Brussels issued a declaration listing specific weapons and strategies which should be banned.

o The use of poison or poisoned weapons.

o Murder by treachery of individuals belonging to the hostile nation or army.

o Murder of an antagonist who, having laid down his arms, or having no longer the means of defending himself, has surrendered at discretion.

o The declaration that no quarter will be given.

o The use of arms, projectiles, or substances which may cause unnecessary suffering, as well as the use of projectiles prohibited by the Declaration of St. Petersburg in 1868. Abuse of the flag, or the military insignia or uniform of the enemy, as well as the distinctive badges of the Geneva Convention.[6]

The United States was not a signator to this Declaration. It was believed to have been important enough, however, for the Secretary-General of the United Nations, in his report on human rights in armed conflict, November 10, 1969, to urge that the United States and other nations which had not signed the Brussels Declaration do so.

THE GENEVA PROTOCOL OF 1925

On June 17, 1925, at Geneva, representatives from forty-four nations issued a "Protocol for the Prohibition of Poisonous Gases and Bacteriological Methods of Warfare." Its major premise was,

Whereas the use in war of asphyxiating, poisonous or other gases, and of all analogous liquids, materials or devices, has been justly condemned by the general opinion of the civilized world. The High Contracting Parties accept this prohibition, agree to extend this prohibition to the use of bacteriological methods of warfare.[7]

Neither the United States nor Great Britain was a signator. Indeed, the distinguished British scientist, J.B.S. Haldane, wrote a pamphlet to "prove" that gas warfare was more humane than any other kind.[8] Great Britain finally ratified the Protocol in 1930. The United States did not do so until 1976. When it did so, it was with the reservations that the United States be permitted to determine what chemicals, gases, or bacteriological weapons were intended to be banned by the Protocol. U.S. leaders took the position that no weapons then in the United States arsenals were prohibited.[9] It should be noted that the United States delegates to the 1925 conference did sign the Protocol, but that the U.S. Senate failed to ratify these signatures.

The failure of the United States to endorse the Geneva Protocol as well as the significant Hague and Geneva declarations proved an embarrassment at the time of the Nuremberg and Tokyo Trials. This underscored the questionable policy of using judges from non-signator nations, when those same policies were the bases for holding the Trials at all. This matter was further exacerbated by the 1976 revisions, under President Nixon, of *The Law of Land Warfare*. The United States, in accepting the 1925 Geneva Protocol, said that they renounced only the "first use" of these banned weapons, and in reprisal the United States believed that it could use them at will. Such an interpretation was not in either the spirit or letter of the Protocol. The implications of the United States qualification cannot be overstated. The U.S. Army, Navy, and Air Force manual on the *Employment of Chemical and Biological Agents* not only listed as part of their standard arsenals Nerve Agent GB, which even the manual affirmed caused convulsions, paralysis, and death,[10] but it also included 32 delivery systems for chemical munitions. Of those the manual classified 21 as producing death, 10 as contaminants, and only 3 as simply incapacitating. This was not an endorsement of the letter or spirit of the Protocol.

UNITED NATIONS DECLARATIONS

The General Assembly of the United Nations issued a "Resolution on Nuclear Weapons," November 24, 1961, Resolution No. 1653, which considered nuclear weapons in the class of poisons, hence covered by the prohibitions of the Geneva Protocol. The declaration stated,

> The use of nuclear and thermonuclear weapons is contrary to the spirit, letter and aims of the United Nations, and, as such, a direct violation of the Charter of the United Nations.[11]

The Resolution pointed out that such weapons caused unnecessary and indiscriminate suffering. They were genocidal weapons. The effects of nuclear radiation were comparable to those of poison gas. Unfortunately, neither the nuclear nor the non-nuclear nations showed much support.

On November 10, 1969 the Secretary-General of the United Nations made a report on human rights in armed conflicts. At that time he recalled the importance of The Hague and Geneva Conventions and Declarations, and especially the Geneva Protocol of 1925. He called on those member nations which had posted reservations to those Conventions to withdraw them. He reminded the member states of U.N. Resolution No. 2444 which had restated that the right to injure the enemy was not unlimited. He reaffirmed U.N. Resolution No. 1653 which had classified nuclear weapons as excessive. He reminded the members that the use of poison and poisoned bullets had been prohibited since the Brussels Declaration of 1874, and he maintained, contrary to American official opinion, that the Geneva Protocol had prohibited *all* chemical, gas, and bacteriological warfare, whether in first strike or in reprisal. He made special reference to napalm, both because it was an incendiary and caused asphyxiation like a gas, and because it caused unnecessary suffering. He observed that it was a sad commentary that certain major powers were so unclear on the very issues which at the time of Nuremberg had seemed so obvious.

The failure of the Genocide Convention issued by the U.N. General Assembly, December 20, 1948, to be approved by the U.S. Senate symbolized the degree to which all such resolutions and declarations had failed to achieve law or rule status. President Truman urged the Senate to adopt the Genocide Convention in a letter to the Senate June 16, 1949.[12]No action was taken by the Congress by the time of adjournment. The matter was not raised during the eight years of President Eisenhower's term of office. Indeed, John Foster Dulles, his Secretary of State, promised that the Genocide Convention would never be brought to the Senate during his term of office. The matter lay dormant during the administrations of both Kennedy and Johnson. Not until President Richard Nixon wrote to the Senate February 19, 1970 urging the Senate to approve the Genocide Convention was the matter taken up again for discussion and debate by the Senate Subcommittee on Foreign Relations during the period April 24, 27, and May 22, 1970.[13] Speaking in favor of adoption was Professor Richard N. Gardner on behalf of the "Ad Hoc Committee on Human Rights and Genocide Treaties." This group represented fifty-two labor, religious, civic and nationality groups.[14] A number of congresspersons, lawyers, and civic leaders testified on behalf of adoption. In opposition, the major force leading to the failure of the Senate even to vote on the matter was the American Bar Association (ABA). It should be noted that the opposition narrowly passed by a vote of 130 to 126. Also speaking against the Genocide Convention were "The Liberty Lobby," "The National Socialist White People's Party," and the "American Coalition of Patriotic Societies," representing 91 essentially anti-Communist groups.[15] Senator Sam J. Ervin, Jr. was particularly opposed. A summary of their fears was given by Senator Proxmire who dismissed all such arguments as specious.[16] At the close of the Hearings the Subcommittee, by a vote of 10 to 2, presented the matter to the Senate December 8, 1970. Congress failed to act prior to the adjournment of the 91st Congress. When Congress reconvened the Subcommittee took the matter up for further discussion March 10, 1971.[17] While the American Bar Association remained opposed, several subsections of that organization presented favorable reports on behalf of the Convention. Senator Ervin was permitted further testimony in opposition, and opposition was given by the Cardinal Mindszenty Foundation which accused the support as coming from the Communist Party. Again the matter was referred to the Senate and again no action was taken.

A change in constituency of the ABA prompted a new stand in favor of adoption of the Genocide Convention and President Jimmy Carter in a letter dated May 23, 1977 urged the Senate to adopt.[18] In addition to the support of the American Bar Association, affirmative letters came from the Defense Department, William F. Buckley, Jr. and a large number of political leaders among whom was Arthur J. Goldberg speaking on behalf of the Ad Hoc Committee on Human Rights and Genocide Treaties. Opposition was voiced again by the "Liberty Lobby" and Senator Jesse Helms of North Carolina added his opposition to that of Senator Sam Ervin. Finally on April 13, 1988 a "Genocide Convention Implementation Act" was submitted to the Committee of the Whole House by the Committee of the Judiciary. It was passed with some reservations and Title 18, United States Code added a Chapter 50A making Genocide a U.S. offense.[19]

Coming so close after the War Crimes Trials the fate of the Genocide Convention revealed something about American sentiment concerning the expectation that no further such trials would occur. Discussion in the U.S. Senate revealed fears that American troops might themselves be prosecuted for crimes and the judges might not be American. Article I of the Genocide Convention had defined genocide in accordance with the Nuremberg Charter.

Genocide means any of the following acts committed with intent to destroy, in whole or in part, a national, ethnical, racial, or religious group.[20]

Genocidal acts included killing, causing severe bodily damage, mental harm, birth prevention, the forcible transfer of children to some other group, and the deliberate lowering of living standards so as to exterminate that group. Article III added that genocidal acts included the conspiracy to commit genocide, complicity in the act, and the attempt to do so. Article IV warned that the guilty would be punished whether they were rulers, lesser officials, or common soldiers or civilians. Yet, this was the Convention which the U.S. Senate had refused to endorse for forty years.

DO THESE CONGRESSES GIVE US LAWS OF WAR?

Do conventions and resolutions such as these constitute laws of war? International law texts base such laws of war on treaties and custom. With respect to the laws of war in particular, they were said to be derived from practices which had become generally enough followed to be called customs. These customs were the bases of laws of war. "Usages of war" lacked the universality, uniformity, and element of obligation required for laws. L. Oppenheim summed up this matter in his definition of laws of war as, "generally binding customs and international treaties."[21] How international must a treaty be before it can be a basis for a law of war? The 1864 Geneva Conventions were endorsed by only twelve participant nations. Did these constitute a treaty or a basis for law? There were twenty-six nations at the first Hague Congress, and no Declaration or Convention ever had the signature of all of the participants. Was there a point at which it could properly be said that The Hague Conventions were custom? If nations could be excused by not signing, were these really laws? United Nations Resolutions had far more nations in agreement than any convention of The Hague or Geneva, yet none of them was ever listed as evidence of laws of war by the U.S. Army manual, *The Law of Land Warfare*

The charge that the Germans and Japanese had been guilty of crimes against the peace had even less basis in history. The Nuremberg Tribunal appealed to the Paris Peace Pact of August 27. 1928. The essence of that pact was contained in the first Article.

The High Contracting Parties solemnly declare, in the names of their respective peoples, that they condemn recourse to war for the solution of international controversies and renounce it as an instrument of national policy in their relations with each other.[22]

The French held a widely expressed reservation that if any country violated this pledge, then all countries were automatically released from their pledge. This made the Pact, at most, a renunciation of "first strike" war, while reserving the "second strike" option. It was assumed, of course, that the Pact did not affect the national right to self-defense. In spite of this, the Nuremberg Courts referred to the Pact as having outlawed war, or at least aggressive war. The Pact did not, however, mention "aggressive war," nor was it ever seriously believed by any of its signators that it represented a formal commitment to renounce war as a method. Nations had considered this Pact to be a sentimental humanitarian wish. No nation took steps to beat its swords into plowshares as a consequence of the Pact.

In spite of this, Oppenheim listed both the United Nations Charter and the Paris Pact as official renunciations of war as a national policy.[23] Nonetheless, as Oppenheim pointed out in his second volume, this renunciation had qualifications. The Pact outlawed war as a general policy, but did not outlaw it as a means for national defense.[24] At the Nuremberg and Tokyo Trials it had been argued that Japan and Germany had waged war as part of a national policy and not for reasons of national defense. Yet, it is not clear how a nation would wage war if not as part of its national policy.

The case for laws of war was undermined by the ubiquitous fact that the doctrine of military necessity and the right of reprisal took precedence over any declarations and conventions of peace congresses. Oppenheim had claimed that only usages of war could be dismissed in the name of military necessity. Customs and the laws they entailed could not be dismissed.[25] The distinction, however, between usage and custom was uninformative as long as military necessity determined what was usage and what was custom. Both The Hague and Geneva prohibitions could be avoided under military duress. Hague rules forbade shooting at disabled soldiers. No comparable rule prohibited shooting at disabled airplanes. Hague had prohibited incendiary or explosive bullets against foot soldiers, but it was accepted custom to use them against aircraft. If Oppenheim were correct in the claim that only usages could be dismissed in the name of necessity, military practice implied that no customs existed. Every practice was mere usage.

It was hoped at the Geneva Conferences that some acts of war would be prohibited because they were inhumane, and not simply because they were militarily redundant. It made no humanitarian sense to claim that the first use of a weapon was criminal while accepting the second use. This seemed especially clear in the case of reprisal bombings of civilian centers. Since the official American positions on these matters are best documented in the military manuals, let us turn to them. We will concentrate on the U.S. Army manuals for several reasons. First, because there is nothing comparable for other branches of the military. Second, because they are readily available and amenable to alteration. We may safely presume that other nations have comparable documents. And third, because they best represent our administrative position toward the importance and relevance of these post-World War II Trials.

NOTES

1. *Geneva Convention of 1864.* Executive Document No. 177. 47th
    Congress, 1st Session. U.S. Senate. Washington, March 3, 1882.

2. *Ibid.*

3. *Conference for the Revision of the Geneva Convention of 1906* (Geneva,
    1930).

4. International Committee of the Red Cross, *The Geneva Conventions
    of August 12, 1949* (Geneva, 1949).

5. James Brown Scott (ed.), *The Hague Conventions and Declarations
    of 1899 and 1907* (New York: Oxford University Press, 1915).

6. Leon Friedman, *The Law of War* (New York: Random House, 1972),
    p. 196.

7. Philip John Noel-Baker, *The Geneva Protocol for the Pacific Settle-
    ment of International Disputes* (London: P.S. King and Sons, 1925).

8. J.B.S. Haldane, *Callinicus: A Defense of Chemical Warfare* (New York:
    Garland Publishing Company, 1972).

9. Cf. Change No. 1, July 15, 1976. Paragraphs 38b and c of *The
    Law of Land Warfare.*

10. *Field Manual 11-3*. March 31, 1966. Ch. II, paragraph 7.

11. Cf. Friedman, *The Law of War*.

12. *Genocide Convention*. Hearings before A Subcommittee of the
    Committee on Foreign Relations United States Senate, ninety-first
    Congress, April 24, 17, and May 22, 1970, pp.2-3 (Washington, D.C.,
    1970)

13. *Ibid.*, p. 12.

14. *Ibid.*, pp. 113-114.

15. *Ibid.*, pp. 185-187.

16. *Ibid.*, pp. 19f.

17. *Genocide Convention*. Hearing before A Subcommittee on Foreign Relations United States Senate, Ninety-Second Congress, March 10, 1971 (Washington, D.C., 1971).

18. *Genocide Convention*. Hearings Before The Committee on Foreign Relations United States Senate, Ninety-Fifth Congress, May 24 and 26, 1977. p. 54 (Washington, 1977).

19. *Genocide Convention Implementation Act of 1988*, 100th Congress, 2nd Session, House of Representatives, Report 100-566.

20. Cf. Friedman, *The Law of War*.

21. L. Oppenheim, *International Law: A Treatise* (London: Longmans, 1952), Vol. II, paragraph 69, p..232.

22. *Renunciation of War Treaty*. Paris, August 27, 1928. U.S. Government Printing Office, 1928.

23. Oppenheim, *International Law*, Vol. I, paragraph 499, p. 892.

24. *Ibid.*, Vol. II, paragraph 52, footnote p. 182.

25. *Ibid.*, Vol. II, paragraph 69, p. 233.

Chapter 5
MILITARY MANUALS
AND THE LAWS OF WAR

The military manuals exhibit the perennial tension that has existed between the prohibitions of congresses and the instructions given to soldiers. After all, the primary aim of the military strategist was to lead his troops to victory. Even the remarks of St. Augustine and St. Thomas concerning the requirements of just war theory were modified by their assumption that wars were to be won. Pope Innocent III might denounce the crossbow as excessive, but the interest of soldiers was to win battles, not to worry about what weapons they might be using. Knights in formal combat commonly chose their weapons proportional to the weapons of their adversaries, but soldiers were not knights in any sense of the term. Fichte's objection against the use of snipers because it was unsporting awoke no military concern as long as sniping was militarily ineffective.[1] Long before the writing of the first American military manuals concerned with battle strategy and permissible weapons, military theorists had considered the role of the soldier as a professional whose primary task was to wage wars to a successful conclusion. Hindrances to that end, based on any so-called humane concerns, were customarily rejected or ignored out of hand.

MILITARY THEORY

With rare exceptions, during the era of knighthood, military theory, at least in the West, was divorced from those traditions of just war theory which might concern themselves with matters of proportionality. Sun Tzu was an exception to an otherwise conventional dichotomy between how to wage war militarily and the morality of the means used to accomplish this end to victory. Sun Tzu had observed,

> War is a matter of vital importance to the State; the province of life or death; the road to survival or ruin. It is mandatory that it be studied.[2]

Ideally, he maintained, the wise commander would hope to overthrow the enemy without recourse to war. From this premise, he noted,

> Generally in war the best policy is to take the State intact....To capture the enemy's army is better than to destroy it....To subdue the enemy without fighting is the acme of skill.[3]

If an enemy could not be overcome by nonviolent means, the wise commander fought in such a way as to achieve victory in the shortest time, at the least cost in lives and effort, and inflicting the fewest casualties. Parsimony governed the wise commander, less because his arms were in short supply, than because he regretted the needless waste of human lives.

In the West, however, concern with moral matters was not part of the mainstream of military theory. Professional soldiers were worried about victory. Moral matters were the province of theologians or philosophers. Even during the medieval period when rulers and commanders were commonly the same persons, wars were conducted, "according to no set legal, logistical, or tactical formulae."[4] Much thought had been given to military strategy, but no thought commensurate with the issues of laws or limits.

Carl von Clausewitz was the paradigm of the Western military thinkers, and his ideas on war had been the dominant ones ever since he first wrote in the nineteenth century. Although his writing covered a wide variety of matters, his disciples concentrated on his justification of total war. War, said Clausewitz, was "an act of violence pushed to its utmost bounds."[5] His interests were prudential and he considered the restrictions posed by international laws as "hardly worth mentioning."[6] Philanthropy in war discussions was,

> an error which must be extirpated, for in such dangerous things as War, the errors which proceed from the spirit of benevolence are of the worst.[7]

Indeed, "to introduce into the philosophy of war itself a principle of moderation would be an absurdity."[8] The failure to use maximum force at the soonest possible time was simply poor military strategy. The military incentive was to escalate war to its most violent as soon as possible. While Clausewitz had noted that the ends of war should govern the amount of sacrifice an army should be willing to make, no suggestion was intended of surrender in cases where the ends seemed trivial.

Military theorists did not consider that the aims of their nation state might ever be too unworthy to be pursued or defended. Herman Kahn was typical in this regard when he undertook to think "the unthinkable." He considered that a million American lives was not too great a price to pay in a nuclear exchange with the Soviet Union if it would avoid a Soviet takeover. No World War I or II leader seemed to calculate whether the cost in human life would be excessive. A general indifference to the human cost appears in Kahn's observation that "the weapons and tactics for a genuinely suicidal thermonuclear war can and may be developed and used."[9] Senator Russell, confronted by the possibility that in a nuclear exchange most of the American population might be killed, remarked with remarkable aplomb that, "If we have to start all over again with Adam and Eve, then I want them to be Americans."[10] General Patton had observed in a similar vein,

> There can never be too many projectiles in battle. Whether they are thrown by cannon, rockets, or recoilless devices is immaterial. The purpose is to deluge the enemy with fire.[11]

Vice Admiral W.L. Rodgers,USN, (Ret.) surmised that it was unlikely that a military leader would ever give up an effective way of attacking and subduing an enemy by the bare plea of "humanity."[12] Comments such as these make it clear that efforts to propose that there are or should be laws of war limiting what armies are permitted to do will not be welcomed by the military establishment.

Giulio Douhet was the first serious military spokesperson on the general theory of aerial warfare. His book, *Command of the Air*, appeared in 1921. He rejected the concept that it was the function of air forces to attack enemy troops, but claimed, on the contrary, that the primary objective was harassment of the civilian populations. To this end he recommended three kinds of bombs: explosives to batter the target, incendiaries to set fire to the remains, and poison gas to prevent fire fighters from extinguishing the blaze thus produced. His views were standard practice in World War II and in the Vietnam War. Citizens were now the major target in war, and their deaths were not incidental nor unintended.

This was confirmed at the Casablanca Conference in January, 1943. At that time indiscriminate bombing was made official policy. Soldiers were told,

> Your primary object will be the progressive destruction of the German military, industrial and economic system, and the undermining of the morale of the German people.[13]

Lieutenant-General E.L.M. Burns remarked at the time,

> Undermining morale sounds a nice gentle persuasive way of
> waging war, until one realises that it means killing civilian
> men, women, and children indiscriminately.[14]

Even the 1956 edition of *The Law of Land Warfare* continued to advise
the soldier that

> there is no prohibition of general application against bom-
> bardment from the air of combatant troops, defended places,
> or other legitimate military objectives.[15]

Is any sense of proportionality present in this military enterprise? A
military writer raised the understandable and unanswerable query,

> The airman might properly ask how he is to know, flying off
> the wing of his flight commander at 30,000 feet, at night, or
> over a solid covering of clouds whether the damage his
> bombs will inflict will meet the test of proportionality.[16]

The military understanding of these matters for the United States
Army was presented in five versions of the official U.S. Army manual
since 1863. These manuals were titled:

o *General Orders 100: Instructions for the Government of
   Armies of the United States in the Field*, (1863).

o *Rules of Land Warfare*, (1914).

o *Rules of Land Warfare*, (1934).

o *Rules of Land Warfare*, (1940). Revision of the section on
   superior orders, (1944).

o *The Law of Land Warfare*, (1956). Revision of the section
   on Chemical/Biological warfare, (1976).

If laws of war were admitted to exist and if limits were acknow-
ledged to what soldiers should be allowed to do, the manuals specified
the official United States position. At the same time, the manuals
evidenced the current military doctrine which doubts that laws of war
should be admitted to exist. Each subsequent edition made reference
to the relevant international peace congresses, beginning with the first

International Red Cross conference of 1864, and continuing through the Conference of St. Petersburg of 1868, Brussels in 1874, The Hague Conferences of 1899 and 1907, and additional International Red Cross Conferences of 1906, 1925, 1929, and 1949. In each case the manual identified which declarations of the congresses were accepted by the United States, and which were rejected, with the implication that the United States did not consider itself bound by any declaration which it had not endorsed. In those cases where Hague or Geneva prohibitions were rejected the manuals appealed to three military doctrines which were used to justify this rejection. These were:

o The doctrine of military necessity, which affirmed that no militarily useful strategy or weapon should ever be prohibited on the mere grounds that they were inhumane.

o The principle of the right of reprisal which allowed an army to use an otherwise forbidden weapon or strategy against an enemy which had first used such against that army.

o The obligation of the soldier to obey superior orders.

THE DOCTRINE OF MILITARY NECESSITY

The notion of military necessity was the basic premise of having an army at all. The function of armies was to win wars, and it followed that they should be permitted to do whatever would bring about success. While some military concern had centered on needless killing or devastation not required for victory, the objection was more a matter of prudence than of humanitarian scruples. International jurists accepted the doctrine as consistent with the military enterprise. While medieval church councils had occasionally attempted to prohibit some weapon or strategy on humanitarian grounds, military practice was to accept only such prohibitions as referred to weapons or strategies which were ineffective or unnecessary. The primary humanitarian concern with this doctrine was whether military necessity justified abandoning the combatant-non-combatant distinction. Was military necessity limited, on humanitarian grounds, from acts which denied that any persons were innocents?

The first U.S. Army manual, *General Orders 100*, written by Professor Francis Lieber under orders from President Lincoln and Secretary of War Stanton, accepted the doctrine that whatever was militarily necessary should not be forbidden. The task, then, was to determine what was militarily necessary in any particular case. The manual stated that military necessity named, "those measures which are indispensable for securing the ends of war and which are lawful according to the modern law and usages of war."[17] All destruction was permitted if such destruction was "unavoidable."[18] However, military necessity did not permit "suffering for the sake of suffering."[19] To this end it was forbidden to use torture to extract information, to use poisons, or to commit acts of perfidy. Were the above not permitted because they were militarily unnecessary? Or were they unlawful "according to the modern law and usages of war?"

The 1914 version titled *Rules of Land Warfare* reprinted the identical phrases of the 1863 manual as to the meaning of military necessity and the existence of laws or usages of war. The Hague Conferences of 1899 and 1907 had been held and recommendations had been issued to the effect that the means of injuring the enemy were not without limit. Among those "limits" was The Hague Declaration prohibiting the dropping of projectiles from balloons. The manual, however, dismissed the declaration as being "of comparatively little value."[20] The manual also reminded the soldier that the U.S. Army was under no limitations, in spite of The Hague recommendations, with respect to the use of gas and noxious chemicals. The soldier was further advised that the U.S. arsenals contained no weapons which might cause "unnecessarily cruel wounds." The Hague had issued a declaration against causing such wounds and had prohibited the use of gas, noxious chemicals, and expanding bullets because they did cause cruel wounds. The U.S. was not a signator either to the prohibition against gas and noxious chemicals or to the ban against expanding bullets. Nonetheless, the manual asserted that it still satisfied The Hague limitation against weapons which caused such "unnecessarily cruel wounds."[21] Neither The Hague nor the manual had a cruelty calculus by which it could be determined when the offense had been committed. Indeed, the only list of prohibited weapons as far as the 1914 military manual was concerned was identical to the list in the 1863 manual, namely, lances with barbed tips, irregularly shaped bullets, or projectiles filled with glass or irritants.

Did military necessity justify the bombing of essentially civilian targets? The 1863 version had urged officers, where feasible, to let an enemy know that a bombardment was going to occur where danger existed of civilian casualties. This advice was, however, conditioned by the premise that where surprise would be a military advantage, the advance warning could be eliminated.[22] The task undertaken in the 1914 edition was to define when a place might be considered to be defended as opposed to undefended. The 1914 edition said that a place was defended when 1) it was a fort, 2) it was a town surrounded by forts, or 3) it was a place either occupied by a military force or through which a military force was passing.[23]

Both the 1934 and 1940 versions contained the same advice and the same qualifications. Even the 1956 version, *The Law of Land Warfare*, added no new element, although it did urge that, "civilians must not be made the object of attack directed exclusively against them."[24] Several factors made it unlikely that any attack would ever be directed "exclusively" against civilians. Bombs were now so vast in their destruction that the airman could always claim that some military target would be hit no matter where he released his explosives. Obviously some civilian target would also be inevitably destroyed. Indeed, in guerrilla warfare every place became a proper target. Military writers now could conclude that it was "doubtful whether it is feasible to observe the rules of either traditional or modern war law."[25] "Unnecessary suffering" or "superfluous injury", both of which were to be avoided, remained a mystery. Given military necessity, and the fact that it was always interpreted by the military, none of these attempts at limitation could ever succeed. The manual advised the soldier

> what weapons cause "unnecessary injury" can only be determined in the light of the practice of States from refraining from the use of a given weapon.[26]

This simply meant that if a weapon was in the arsenal, then it did not cause "unnecessary injury." How could the soldier figure out why barbed spears should be overly injurious while napalm and fragmentation bombs were not? Since the U.S. had rejected the prohibition against gas and noxious chemicals, the American position was that while lances with barbed tips were excessive, gas and noxious chemicals were not. This doctrine, that whatever is militarily useful, hence, necessary, must always be permitted will always frustrate efforts to set limits. Little reason from the past leads us to expect that the military will limit itself, and little reason exists for hope that some force outside the military will successfully impose limits on it.

THE RIGHT OF REPRISAL

This doctrine expressed an ultimate appeal to the doctrine of military necessity. The current Army manual, *The Law of Land Warfare*, defined such acts.

> Reprisals are acts of retaliation in the form of conduct which would otherwise be unlawful...for the purpose of forcing future compliance with recognized rules of civilized warfare.[27]

The manual noted that the reprised act should not exceed in violence the initial offense, but that it need not be the same kind of act.[28] The problem was to know when a reprisal was proper, as well as to measure if the reprisal was proportional to the original offense. The Geneva Convention of 1949 forbade reprisals altogether. This matter came up at the Nuremberg Trials since the lawyers for the accused Germans had occasion to claim that some of their supposed offenses were legitimate reprisals. The Nuremberg judges had two options: to deny that the victims of extermination had committed any act warranting reprisal, or to argue that the reprisal was disproportionate to the alleged offense. In the Trial of Wilhelm List and Others the accused were indicted for having shot hostages without first conducting a court martial to determine that an offense had been committed. In the List Case the Court had ruled that shooting 50 to 100 Communists for every German slain was excessive. However, the Court did not determine what a proper number of slain Communists would have been. With what number did the reprised act exceed in violence the original offense? The doctrine of the right of reprisal was, as Evelyn Speyer Colbert observed, "a reflection both of the absence of law enforcing machinery in international law and of desire of states to justify their acts."[29] Oppenheim, while accepting the right of reprisals, noted that they were commonly used as a "convenient cloak for violations of international law."[30] This situation was bound to exist given that each sovereign nation made its own assessment as to whether a crime had been committed and whether a reprisal was justified. Oppenheim concluded,

> In face of the arbitrariness with which, according to the present state of International Law, resort can be had to reprisals, the question arises as to the feasibility of an agreement upon some rules governing resort to them in time of war.[31]

The Hague did not deal with the issue of reprisals, while Geneva forbade them altogether.

There is serious doubt whether any of the U.S. Army manuals ever gave the soldier sufficient advice on either military necessity or reprisal. The rank and file needed to obey orders, and they never had occasion even to be informed. The officers who gave the orders, however, clearly needed some instruction as to the legitimacy of a reprisal or the necessity of a military act. Article I of the 1907 Hague "Convention Respecting Laws and Customs of War" had required that the Contracting Powers issue instructions to their respective armed forces. Two interpretations were given to this recommendation. The first was that whatever instructions were given were to be in accord with the Convention. Thus, if no instructions were given at all, the Convention would not have been violated. The other interpretation was that instructions must be given, and that they must be in accord with the Convention. At the very least, a copy of *Rules of Land Warfare* should have been in the possession of all soldiers in a position to give orders during the two World Wars, and a copy of *The Law of Land Warfare* should have been distributed prior to the Vietnam War to both those who gave orders and those expected to obey them. The evidence was, however, that such manuals have been consistently out of print and unavailable so that soldiers, generally, have never been issued instructions in the form of the manual or otherwise. Soldiers got no such training in boot camp, nor were officers trained at military colleges on the subject with any degree of thoroughness. The judges at Nuremberg soon discovered this, if they were not previously aware of the fact, that there were no military instructions which forbade extermination camps, although there were ample guidelines from both The Hague and Geneva declarations which forbade war on civilians and the maltreatment of prisoners.

MUST SUPERIOR ORDERS BE OBEYED?

Until 1944 the U.S. Army manuals assumed that soldiers were obligated to obey the orders of their military superiors. When they did so, they were protected from prosecution even when their acts were criminal in terms of the laws of the land. After all, most of what armies do in war would be illegal. Both ancient and medieval theorists granted this immunity to soldiers in uniform, and at war, when they were following superior military orders. When the U.S. Army prosecuted certain of its soldiers for war crimes following the Philippine War, it was because, either they had not been ordered to do what they did, or because the higher authority who gave the order did so improperly. Sooner or later in the military system we come to the originator of the order. That person cannot plead superior orders, although he might argue effectively that he had good reason for believing that such an order would be consistent with past policy.

One of the reasons for the writing of the first U.S. Army manual, *General Orders 100*, was that officers in the field were giving orders to their subordinates which were believed to be contrary to "laws of war." Certain Northern officers were permitting their soldiers to pillage, kill after surrender, ignore the combatant-non-combatant distinction, and to take as personal booty the private possessions of the Confederate citizenry. Paragraph 44 of this first manual deplored all such acts and by so doing advised officers in the field to cease allowing their subordinates to commit these deeds and to cease committing these deeds themselves. This was the official position in 1914 with the publication of *Rules of Land Warfare*. Paragraph 366 stated,

> Individuals of the armed forces will not be punished for these offenses in case they are committed under the orders or sanction of their government or commanders. The commanders ordering the commission of such acts, or under whose authority they are committed by their troops, may be punished by the belligerent into whose hands they may fall.

The actions of the Court Martial following the Philippine War showed that the U.S. Army itself may punish the offending officers, but it was a drastic concession to grant that the enemy, if victorious, could so prosecute these officers. Indeed, the 1934 and 1940 editions of *Rules of Land Warfare* deleted this reference to what belligerent victors might be allowed to do.

In anticipation of the war crimes trials the Allies, and the U.S. in particular, altered this reference to superior orders essentially to disallow this appeal by German or Japanese soldiers. Paragraph 345 of the 1940 Army manual, referring to Hague IV, article 3, now cautioned soldiers,

> Individuals and organizations who violate the accepted laws and customs of war may be punished therefore. However, the fact that the acts complained of were done pursuant to orders of a superior or government sanction may be taken into consideration in determining culpability, either by way of defense or in mitigation of punishment. The person giving such orders may also be punished.

This was further altered in 1956 in *The Law of Land Warfare*, article 501.

> In some cases, military commanders may be responsible for war crimes committed by subordinate members of the armed forces, or other persons subject to their control. Thus, for instance, when troops commit massacres and atrocities against the civilian population of occupied territory or against prisoners of war, the responsibility may rest not only with the actual perpetrators but also with the commander.

Paragraph 509 stated specifically that if a law of war has been violated pursuant to following the orders of a superior, the act is still criminal. This is qualified by the allowance of ignorance on the part of the subordinate as to what orders he is obligated to obey. It is less clear whether the commander may also plead ignorance as to which orders he is forbidden to give. This ambiguity played a major role in the failure to prosecute all of the original twenty eight officers and two enlisted men first cited by the Peers Commission following the events at My Lai and Son My, and was one of the major reasons why only three relatively inferior rank soldiers were ultimately tried. While Paragraphs 502 and 504 list some of the specific acts which officers are forbidden to require, it still remained unclear where officers would receive this training so that they would know in the field where to draw the line.

FORBIDDEN STRATEGIES AND WEAPONS

If there were no forbidden strategies or weapons, there would be no war crimes, since everything would be permitted. The efforts to set limits to the means by which wars were waged came, primarily, from sources outside the military tradition. Early Roman Catholic Church Councils had proposed bans on the use of incendiaries, poisons, and the crossbow, as well as against the strategy of making deliberate war on civilians or of declaring that a war would be fought with "no quarter." The frequency with which successive councils needed to restate these bans indicated the general failure of armies to follow their recommendations. In the nineteenth and twentieth centuries the task of proposing limits came from international peace congresses such as those at Geneva, The Hague, St. Petersburg, and Brussels. The U.S. Army manuals, beginning with the first, *General Orders 100*, made reference to these efforts. From the perspective of the Nuremberg Trials, which needed to be able to demonstrate that there were limits to what could be sanctioned in war, the Army manuals presented a most inadequate basis.

Incendiaries

Prohibitions against the use of incendiaries in war went back to ancient times. In the middle ages incendiaries were the most frequently mentioned forbidden weapons. While each Army manual insisted that it did not endorse the use of any weapon which caused "unnecessary suffering" or "superfluous injury" the matter of whether incendiaries were in the class of offenders was strenuously denied. Both the conference at St. Petersburg in 1868 and those at The Hague in 1899 and 1907 (especially in Article XXIII) deplored the use of weapons causing excessive injury or suffering. This same prohibition against excessive weapons was affirmed in *Rules of Land Warfare* (1914), Paragraph 184; *Rules of Land Warfare* (1934 and 1940), Paragraph 34; and *The Law of Land Warfare* (1956), Paragraph 41. By the time of the 1956 manual a number of sophisticated incendiaries were in the American arsenals, including flamethrowers and napalm. In spite of long tradition against incendiaries, and in spite of successive Geneva Conventions against their use, the current Army Manual, *The Law of Land Warfare*, stated in Paragraph 36,

> The use of weapons which employ fire, such as tracer ammunition, flamethrowers, napalm and other incendiary agents, against targets requiring their use is not violative of international law. They should not, however, be employed in such a way as to cause unnecessary suffering to individuals.

The assertion that napalm and flamethrowers might be used in such ways as not to cause unnecessary suffering was difficult to reconcile with studies made on the effects of napalm in particular. The Secretary-General of the United Nations in 1969 urged that a study be made of the medical consequences of the use of incendiaries like napalm. In 1972 there was published *The United Nations Study on Incendiary Weapons and All Aspects of Their Use* (U.N. Document No. A-8803). This led to a U.N. Resolution banning napalm and other incendiaries. The General Assembly passed the Resolution by a vote of 99 yea, 0 nay, and 15 abstentions. A similar Resolution was passed by the U.N. in 1981 banning "particularly inhumane weapons" which included fragmentation bombs, incendiaries, and booby traps. The United States did not sign either Resolution. The presumption of the manual that incendiaries could be used without causing unnecessary suffering was no help at the time of the Nuremberg Trials against the Germans for having used the cremating ovens. Were we supposed to imagine that such incendiary ovens could not be used without causing unnecessary suffering, while napalm and flame throwers could?

Chemical/Biological Weapons

The Congress at Brussels in 1874 and The Hague Conferences of 1899 and 1907 forbade deleterious gases which both groups listed as poisons. Indeed *General Orders 100* had affirmed that American troops did not use poisons.

> The use of poison in any manner, be it to poison wells, or food or arms, is wholly excluded from modern warfare. He

that uses it puts himself out of the pale of the law and usages of war. (Paragraph 70)

The 1914 *Rules of Land Warfare* cited Hague Resolution XXIII that it was "especially forbidden" to use poison or poisoned weapons. Unfortunately, the U.S. did not consider gases and chemicals as poisons. The same ambiguous situation still existed in the 1934 and 1940 editions of *Rules of Land Warfare*, which stated in Paragraph 28 that the U.S. was not a party to any treaty which prohibited the use of gases or noxious chemicals. Even the 1956 *The Law of Land Warfare* reaffirmed that the U.S. was not a party to any treaty banning gases or chemicals. While the 1925 Geneva Protocol had banned gases, noxious chemicals, as well as bacteriological weapons, it was still the case in the 1956 edition that the U.S. claimed that since it had not been a signator, it was not bound to obey the prohibition. In Army Pamphlet 21-1, 1956, *Treaties Governing Land Warfare*, the soldier was assured that his army was not bound by any protocols limiting the use of gases or chemicals. In 1955 the Secretary of the Army urged that gases and chemicals be listed as conventional weapons, and this in the face of a United Nations commission effort to ban these as "weapons of mass destruction."[32] The Secretary of the Army had argued that these weapons had the advantage of subduing the enemy without destroying property.[33]

In 1976 under President Nixon the Army manual was revised on these matters. The manual stated that the U.S. was now a signator of the 1925 Geneva Protocol, but that it reserved the right to determine which gases and chemicals were banned. Furthermore, contrary to the letter and spirit of the 1925 Protocol, the United States stated that it was only bound to obey the "first use" and could always use them in reprisal. The United States interpretation of what gases and chemicals were still allowable can be seen in the U.S. Army, Navy, and Air Force manual, *Employment of Chemical and Biological Agents*, March 31, 1966. The manual listed as part of the standard arsenal Nerve Agent GB, which the manual stated "caused convulsions, paralysis, and death,"[34] but also included 32 delivery systems for chemical munitions, 21 of which were classified as producing death. General J.H. Rothschild, former head of the Army Chemical Corps, insisted that such weapons were "humane" and that they kept casualties to a minimum.[35] Indeed, the General had stated that if we were to arrange weapons in order of their humaneness, these toxic weapons would be at the top of the list.[36] The remark that such weapons were most humane was qualified by the inconsistent observation that "there is nothing humane about any method of warfare."[37]

Bacteriological weapons were an especially troublesome form of what were called CB (Chemical/Biological) weapons. Indeed, in the

1976 revision of *The Law of Land Warfare*, the manual asserted that the U.S. would not use such weapons either in first or second strike offense. Earlier President Roosevelt had stated that the U.S. would not use biological warfare agents "unless they are first used by our enemies."[38] The Army was not united in its stand on such weapons. The Army Surgeon General, for example, took the position that only the "defensive" aspects of BW should be pursued. However, Brigadier General Rothschild argued so successfully against this position that his organization was permitted to pursue both defensive and offensive research. Quite apart from this, it was surely not clear what the defensive use of BW weapons would look like as compared with the offensive uses. The friction between the Army Medical Corps and the Army Chemical Corps was so great that the Medical Corps refused even to station a team at Fort Detrick, Maryland, the Biological Research Center.

The Chemical Corps produced a pamphlet listing the "most promising antipersonnel agents."[39] The list contained eleven bacteriological agents, five rickettsiae agents, five viral agents, four fungi, and two toxins. While the full list was said to be "classified" it may reasonably be inferred that those unmentioned were not less deadly than those named. The printed list included Bacillus Anthracis, Cholera, Diphtheria, Scrub Typhus, and Nocardia Asteroides. President Ford had ordered the Secretary of Defense to supervise the armed forces to make sure that they abided by the no-first-use mandate. President Nixon announced in 1969 that the U.S. would give up chemical/bacteriological warfare, unless it was defensive. Since the major research centers in the United States for such research continued to operate, were we to assume that all such research was purely defensive? A London Conference on Chemical and Biological Warfare made a survey of the American installations for such research. They included Fort Detrick and Edgewood Arsenal, Maryland; Dugway Proving Ground in Utah; Pine Bluff Arsenal in Arkansas; Denver Rocky Mountain Arsenal; Muscle Shoals in Alabama; the nerve gas plant at Newport, Indiana; the Army Chemical Center and School at Fort McClellan, Alabama; and related activities at Eglin Airforce Base in Florida.[40]

A recent United Nations report reaffirmed the Geneva Protocol position in contradiction to the current American military view. The report stated:

> All weapons of war are destructive of human life, but chemical and bacteriological (biological) weapons stand in a class of their own as armaments which exercise their effects solely on living matter. The idea that bacteriological (biological) weapons could deliberately be used to spread disease

generates a sense of horror. The fact that certain chemical and bacteriological (biological) agents are potentially unconfined in their effects, both in space and time, and that their large-scale use could conceivably have deleterious and irreversible effects on the balance of nature adds to the sense of insecurity and tension which the existence of this class of weapons engenders. Considerations such as these set them into a category of their own in relation to the continuing arms race.[41]

While chemical or bacteriological warfare was not specifically an issue at Nuremberg, there was evidence that the Germans did maltreat prisoners by performing biological experiments on them using both chemical and biological agents. In the Medical Trial conducted under Control Council Law No. 10 the experiments on hapless prisoners were of such a magnitude that of the 23 persons tried, everyone was indicted. The judges at Nuremberg ruled that even military necessity could not justify such experimentation. Indeed, both Geneva and Hague conventions had required that prisoners be as well treated as one's own troops in the field. Sadly the Germans were not alone in such medical experiments. On a limited scale experiments had been carried on in the United States on conscientious objectors during World War II. While these tests may have been made with the consent of the human guinea pigs, they were surely not done with full knowledge of the risks involved.

Yet, at the same time, and without the patriotic pressures which war engenders, the U.S. Department of Defense and the Central Intelligence Agency between 1942 and 1977 conducted chemical, biological, and psychological experiments on American citizens without their knowledge. Hearings at the Subcommittee on Health and Scientific Research of the United States Senate, 95th Congress, First Session revealed that American doctors had followed the example of their Nazi counterparts. Although CIA Director Helms had withheld information from the Subcommittee and even burned records so that the evidence was unavailable, data were sufficient to show what the thrust of these CIA and DOD experiments had been. It was revealed that at least 156 separate experiments had been conducted. Twenty of these were listed as so "classified" that the Subcommittee could not see them. The identified experiments, however, were extremely dismaying. They involved the use on unwitting citizens and soldiers of tularemia, Rift Valley Fever, Bolivian Hemorrhagic Fever, Q Fever, Sandfly Fever, Bubonic Plague, Rocky Mountain Fever, monovalent influenza, and the injection into the bloodstream of whole blood amino acids. The reader might have had some reassurance if these experiments had been carried out by the U.S. Department of Health, although their involvement would have been shocking in itself. But no reasons from the past could assure us that such experiments carried out by the DOD and the CIA would have paid any attention to the safety or rights of the patients. The Senate Subcommittee discovered that 30 experiments had been in the public domain and an additional 141 experiments not in the public domain. The public domain sites included two on the Big Island of Hawaii, two on Oahu in Hawaii, Key West, Florida, San Francisco, Washington, D.C., the National Airport in Washington, D.C., Pennsylvania State Highway No. 10, the Pennsylvania Turnpike, and the Kittatinny and Tuscarora Tunnels.

In a concluding assessment of these experiments, the Committee heard Stephen Weitzman, M.D. of the Department of Microbiology at the State University of New York at Stony Brook. He deplored the carelessness and irresponsibility of both the DOD and the CIA in their conduct. He made three points:

- Large scale and open air testing is unpredictable and dangerous.

- The Army ignored the ethical obligation of informed consent on the part of those who were the guinea pigs.

- Biological warfare research is not in the best interests of the United States, since once the experiments have been concluded the results can be used by terrorists all over the world.[42]

Senator Barry Goldwater, although not present at the meetings, had a statement read into the proceedings.

Certainly there were some unfortunate results particularly in regard to the unwitting participants.... But war itself is an unfortunate thing. [43]

He insisted, further, that those who conducted the experiments were simply patriotic, dedicated American citizens who were given superior orders which they were obligated to obey. But this was the same shocking defense used by the Nazi doctors and the Nuremberg judges had rejected such an excuse as unacceptable.

Edward A. Miller, Assistant Secretary of the Army for Research and Development, assured the Kennedy Subcommittee that the Army had totally destroyed all DOD biological supplies by 1973. President Nixon had requested that this be done in 1969. Yet, in 1977 both the

DOD and the CIA were using biological warfare weapons against American citizens, and this in spite of the 1976 revision of *The Law of Land Warfare*, which reported that the United States had forsworn all bacteriological warfare. In 1978 President Carter announced that the United States would no longer advocate biological warfare, as if from 1969 to 1978 its use was still advocated. It was unfortunate that the CIA and the DOD, with their reputations for secrecy and deception, should have been left in charge of the task of destroying these bacteriological weapons.

The general attitude toward biological warfare in official Army publications has not been helpful in supporting the latest claims that the U.S. has forsaken such warfare. *Military Biology and Biological Warfare Agents*, 3-216 and 355.6, rejected the aforementioned concern that such warfare would be radically worse than previous kinds of warfare. It argued that such warfare is natural since diseases are natural.[44] Whether disease is natural is quite beside the point, since the aim of medicine is to eliminate these natural plagues. Many of the diseases listed in the U.S. arsenals are currently without cure, and this, the Army argues, makes them even better weapons. That such weapons do not discriminate between combatants and non-combatants violates the Geneva and Hague insistence that war not be made deliberately against civilians. Although the United Nations General Assembly, as well as both Geneva and The Hague, had listed biological warfare as violating the most basic laws of humanity, Colonel Bernard J. Brungs seemed to speak for the official military position when he said, "Biological warfare is not prohibited by any universally binding rule of international law."[45]

Nuclear Weapons

The Law of Land Warfare (1956) was the first occasion for the U.S. Army manual to mention atomic or nuclear weapons. The United States had already used two of them on Hiroshima and Nagasaki, August 6 and 9, 1945 and more of them were in the American arsenal for future use. By 1949 the Soviet Union also had nuclear weapons. The British followed in 1952, the French in 1960, the Chinese in 1964, and India in 1974. By 1979 South Africa was suspected to have conducted a nuclear test. The Army manual reference was terse and simple:

> Atomic weapons. The use of explosive "atomic weapons" whether by air, sea, or land forces cannot as such be regarded as violative of international law in the absence of any customary rule of international law or international convention restricting their employment. (Paragraph 35)

The British *The Law of War on Land*, 1958, paragraph 113 stated briefly,

> There is no rule of international law dealing specifically with the use of nuclear weapons. Their use, therefore, is governed by the general principles laid down in this chapter.

We are referred to a footnote to discover what these general principles are, namely, the "compelling dictates of humanity, morality, civilization, and chivalry." Since these dictates are not stated we are left with the conclusion that nuclear weapons may be used as long as one's sense of humanity, morality, civilization, and chivalry are not offended. These two paragraphs make clear that neither American nor British sensibilities are troubled.

L. Oppenheim supported the above two manuals in the 1952 Seventh Edition of his *International Law*.

> In the absence of express international agreement relating to the matter, the question of the legality of the use of atomic weapons must be judged by reference: (a) to existing international instruments relating to the limits of the use of violence in war; (b) to the distinction which many believe to be fundamental, between combatants and non-combatants; and (c) to the principles of humanity, which to some degree, must be regarded as forming part of the law of war.[46]

With regard to international agreements, Oppenheim doubted that either the Declaration of St.Petersburg of 1868 or the Geneva Protocol of 1925 clearly applied, unless it could be shown that nuclear bombs were poisons. With regard to the combatant-non-combatant distinction, Oppenheim noted that since obliteration bombing was done in World War II, with great loss of civilian life, and since it was not treated as a war crime at Nuremberg, it could not be maintained that an international objection existed to the direct and deliberate attack on large numbers of civilians. Since the use of nuclear weapons, thus far, had been an airforce matter, rather than one of armies in the field, Oppenheim recommended that the matter be brought up in a manual in that branch of the military. In this regard he noted,

> There are many who believe that the advent of aircraft and aerial bombing has, so far as their use is concerned, obliterated the distinction between combatants and non-combatants, and that, as has often happened in the past,

restraints of humanity and chivalry must yield to military necessity and to the potentialities of newly discovered weapons of offense.[47]

Both the military manual and the international jurists dismissed the actions of the United Nations, in spite of the fact that their deliberations were far more international than any of the conclusions reached at Geneva or The Hague. When we consider that the Nuremberg judges appealed to The Hague and Geneva conventions as the bases for laws, the breaking of which constituted war crimes in the case of The Hague, and crimes against humanity in the case of Geneva, this dismissal is hard to understand. In 1961 the U.N. General Assembly issued a Resolution banning nuclear weapons as excessive in the sense prescribed by both The Hague and Geneva conventions. There were 77 yea votes, no nay votes, and 29 abstentions (including the United States). At the time, the United Nations paid special attention to what it called weapons of "mass destruction" or "non-directed" weapons. Such weapons, with nuclear weapons as the prime example, harm civilians and military without distinction. The uses of such weapons,

exceed even the scope of war and cause indiscriminate suffering and destruction to mankind and civilization and as such is contrary to the rules of international law and the laws of humanity.[48]

In the 1969 U.N. Resolution on Human Rights In Armed Conflict, nuclear weapons were named as excessive, as abandoning the traditional distinction between combatants and non-combatants, and as causing unnecessary suffering. In 1982 the U.N. passed a Resolution against the manufacture and stockpiling of nuclear weapons. It passed with 147 yea votes and only one nay (the United States). Also in 1982 the U.N. General Assembly issued a Resolution against the use of nuclear weapons as in violation of the letter and spirit of the United Nations Charter. It passed with 121 yea and 19 nay (again including the United States). Even a 1982 Resolution banning nuclear tests in the atmosphere, the sea, and outer space, and a treaty against nuclear proliferation, failed to get U.S. support although it passed 118 yea to 2 nay.

In spite of this strong United Nations consensus American military spokespersons consistently dismissed its Resolutions as having no international status. Captain Fred Bright Jr. wrote in 1965 that the use of atomic weapons cannot be considered in violation of any laws of war. His argument was that a weapon actually in use or in the arsenals of armies of the world, was by that fact a lawful weapon. He concluded that principles of humanity do not prohibit their use. Nor, he said, can there be any, "blanket acceptance or condemnation of nuclear weapons based on the doctrine of proportionality."[49] William V. O'Brien concluded that it was virtually impossible to maintain any humanitarian concern with laws of war since nuclear weapons are accepted.[50] Given this attitude toward nuclear weapons, let alone napalm, gas, and noxious chemicals, it seems meaningless that in the section of *The Law of Land Warfare* dealing with "forbidden weapons" the only weapons clearly banned were those no major nation has in its arsenals. That manual stated:

> Usage had, however, established the illegality of the use of lances with barbed heads, irregular-shaped bullets, and projectiles filled with glass, the use of any substance on bullets that would tend unnecessarily to inflame a wound inflicted on them, and the scoring or filing off of the ends of the hard cases of bullets.[51]

Defenders of nuclear war have attempted to mute the United Nations protest by claiming that they propose only "limited nuclear war." The term "limited" has had an ambiguous history. One interpretation is that any nuclear war in which only one of the two super powers (the Soviet Union and the United States) is involved is by that fact "limited." Since the major thrust of nuclear buildup has been to "protect" the U.S. or the U.S.S.R. from attack by the other, such a "limited nuclear war" is not a very live option. A second interpretation has been to affirm that any war is "limited" if only "tactical" nuclear bombs are used and if the targets are "limited." In any event, while Mutual Assured Destruction (MAD) was the official American policy, it was hoped that all nuclear war would be avoided. Under President Reagan's administration, however, the concept of a winnable nuclear war was introduced, thus removing any hopes based on the MAD hypothesis.

Hanson W. Baldwin, military analyst for the *New York Times*, considered the general question of limited conventional wars. About twenty-three "limited" conventional wars have occurred since World War II, where one but not both of the super powers was involved. Thus "limited conventional wars" are possible. But how about "limited" nuclear wars?

> Thus the lessons of history are plain; limited wars continue even in the shadow of the atomic age.... But history gives us no clue as to whether or not nuclear weapons could be used in such conflicts without spreading them. For in none of the

twenty-three wars since World War II have nuclear weapons of any sort actually been utilized.[52]

In 1979, Admiral Gene R. LaRoque, USN (Ret.), speaking at the first nuclear war conference in Washington, predicted that any limited nuclear war would "inevitably escalate into a full-rate general nuclear war."[53] Even if a so-called "limited" nuclear war were possible, we need to remember that the "limited" nuclear weapons in the U.S. arsenal are still fifty times more powerful than those used against Hiroshima and Nagasaki. Part of the difficulty in comprehending the seriousness of a nuclear war has been a persistent military thesis that nuclear war is just like conventional war, except for an increase in destructive power. This attitude is evidenced in a Defense Department manual, *Radiological Defense*.

> Except for their much greater magnitude, the problems presented by atomic attack are, in many respects, similar to those due to conventional saturation attacks. Although nuclear radiation is a new feature of warfare, the methods of dealing with radioactive contamination involve the same principles as are used for chemical decontamination. The conduct of atomic defense requires no important change in the present military structure.... Even the nuclear radiation, although not heretofore encountered in military weapons, is similar in many respects to chemical warfare from the standpoint of defensive measures. No radical changes in organization are required for military defense against atomic weapons.[54]

Obviously this was not the attitude of the State Department which argued successfully that nuclear war was so horrible that the fear of "mutually assured destruction" would prevent any attempt to use such weapons. Furthermore, the long term consequences of nuclear fallout make it radically different from any other weapon. The U.S. tests on Bikini atoll show that even now the atoll is too contaminated for the residents to be able to move back, and the continued radioactive contamination of vegetable and animal life make this kind of bomb quite different from conventional explosives. Unlike dynamite the consequences of nuclear explosions circle the earth and may last for centuries.

A lone attempt by a court to determine the legality of nuclear weapons occurred in Japan: the Shimoda Case.[55] On December 7, 1963 the District Court of Tokyo issued its decision on behalf of five Japanese individuals who had failed to recover damages from the Japanese government for injuries resulting from the bombings. The

Japanese Court concluded that the United States had violated international law by dropping the bombs. The Court also concluded that the five plaintiffs had a right to compensation. Neither side exercised its right of appeal to a higher court. Apparently the plaintiffs were satisfied that the United States had been found guilty of a war crime. The Japanese government, although persuaded that the U.S. had broken international law, had no intention of paying the plaintiffs itself, and saw no reason to pursue the matter further. The case of the litigants rested on the thesis that international law forbade the use of gas and noxious chemicals, forbade the bombing of civilian centers, the infliction of "unnecessary suffering", and all indiscriminate aerial warfare. Professor Richard A. Falk summarized the findings of the Japanese Court:

o   International law forbids an indiscriminate or blind attack upon an undefended city; Hiroshima and Nagasaki were undefended, therefore, the attacks were illegal.

o   International law only permits, if at all, indiscriminate bombing of a defended city if it is justified by military necessity; no military necessity of sufficient magnitude could be demonstrated here; therefore the attacks were illegal.[56]

Did the Shimoda Case set any precedent? Falk noted in this regard that it would be premature to imagine so. The Shimoda Case by itself could give no answer to whether the use of nuclear weapons, especially in these cases, was a violation of international laws of war. In spite of this, the author reasoned that the case suggested how any future use of nuclear bombs might be judged. Falk observed that just as the Nuremberg Judgment influenced the Eichmann Case, so the Shimoda Case may influence future legal appraisals of the legality of the use of nuclear weapons in war. The U.S. position has been that no international law forbade the nuclear bombings of Japan.[57] It should be noted, further, that the Shimoda Case rejected the argument of the U.S. at that time, that the use of the bombs hastened the surrender of the Japanese nation, and, hence, "saved" lives, including those of the Japanese. Not only did such an American argument rest on an hypothetical situation impossible of testing, but even if the hypothesis were accepted, it would have committed the United States to the theory of total war which justified any act, however horrible, to that end. While the Japanese did surrender after the dropping of the two bombs, the evidence is that had the Allies not insisted on unconditional surrender and had they not insisted that the Japanese give up the role of emperor, Japan would have surrendered long before. It was macabre that the matter of the role of emperor, which had hindered an earlier surrender, was granted to Japan by the Allies when surrender did come. Hypothetical arguments were rejected by the judges at Nuremberg, when accused German leaders had claimed that their actions against the Jews, for example, had "saved" German civilization. Indeed, the Shimoda Case does raise an important question whether the United States can afford to continue to ignore U.N. Resolution No. 1653 which had affirmed:

> The use of nuclear and thermonuclear weapons is contrary to the spirit, letter and aims of the United Nations, and, as such, a direct violation of the Charter of the United Nations....Any State using nuclear and thermonuclear weapons is to be considered as violating the Charter of the United Nations, as acting contrary to the laws of humanity and as committing a crime against mankind and civilization.[58]

If military theory is best expressed in its manuals, then the abyss between prohibition and military licence seems unbridged. We cannot expect Departments of Defense to monitor themselves on matters of laws of war, especially when their political leaders shirk responsibility. If the U.S. Senate refuses to endorse the United Nations Resolutions banning certain weapons of war, we cannot expect a higher sense of humanitarianism to arise from the armed forces. In spite of this state of affairs there have been war crimes trials antedating Nuremberg and Tokyo.

NOTES

1. J.G. Fichte, *The Science of Rights* (Philadelphia: J.B. Lippincott, 1869), p. 484.

2. Sun Tzu, *The Art of War*, (tr.) Samuel B. Griffith (New York: Oxford University Press, 1963), p. 63.

3. *Ibid.*, p.77.

4. John Beeler, *Warfare in Feudal Europe* (Ithaca, N.Y.: Cornell University Press, 1971), p. 247.

5. Carl von Clausewitz, *On War*, (tr) Colonel J.J. Graham (London: Routledge and Kegan Paul, 1966), p. 4.

6. *Ibid.*, Ch. I, paragraph 2.

7. *Ibid.*

8. *Ibid.*

9. Herman Kahn and Anthony J. Wiener, *The Year 2000* (London: Collier-Macmillan, 1967), p. 367.

10. *Anti-Ballistic Missile: Yes or No?* p. 129.

11. George S. Patton, *War as I Knew It* (Boston: Houghton-Mifflin, 1947), p. 357.

12. W.L.Rodgers, "Future International Laws of War," *The American Journal of International Law*. Vol. 33 (July, 1939). p. 441.

13. E.L.M. Burns, *Megamurder* (London: George C. Harrap, 1966) p. 51.

14. *Ibid.*

15. *The Law of Land Warfare*. Ch. II, Section IV, paragraph 42.

16. "The Laws of Land Warfare," *Military Law Review* (September, 1975), p. 299.

17. *General Orders 100*, Section I, paragraph 14.

18. *Ibid.*, Section I, paragraph 15.

19. *Ibid.*, Section I, paragraph 16.

20. *Rules of Land Warfare*, 1914, paragraph 175.

21. *Ibid.*

22. *General Orders 100*, paragraph 19.

23. *Rules of Land Warfare*, paragraphs 212,214,217.

24. *The Law of Land Warfare*, Article 42, paragraph 25.

25. M. Cherif Bassiouni, *A Treatise on International Law* (Springfield, Ill: C.C. Thomas, 1973), Vol. I. p. 185.

26. *The Law of Land Warfare*, paragraph 34b.

27. *Ibid.*, paragraph 497a.

28. *Ibid.*, paragraph 497e.

29. Evelyn Colbert Speyer, *Retaliation in International Law* (New York: King's Crown Press, 1948), p. 1.

30. L. Oppenheim, *International Law* (London: Longmans, 1952), Vol. II, paragraph 247.

31. *Ibid.*, paragraph 250.

32. Philip Noel-Baker, *The Arms Race: A Program for World Disarmament* (London: Stevens and Sons, 1958), p. 315.

33. *Ibid.*, p. 316.

34. Ch. II, paragraph 7.

35. John Cookson and Judith Nottingham, *A Survey of Chemical and Biological Warfare* (London: Sheed and Ward, 1969), p. 337.

36. J.H. Rothschild, "The Facts about Germ and Chemical Warfare," *War/Peace Report* (January, 1962), p. 3.

37. *Ibid.*

38.   Cited in Stephen Rose (ed.), *Chemical and Biological Warfare* (London: George Harrap, 1968), p. 145.

39.   *Technical Manual, TM 3-216.* Cross listed with *Airforce Manual 355-6.* Ch. V, Section 47, p. 43.

40.   Cf. Rose (ed.), *CBW Chemical and Biological Warfare.*

41.   United Nations Report, No. E.69.1.24. *Chemical and Bacteriological (Biological) Weapons and the Effects of Their Possible Use.*

42.   See *Human Drug Testing by the CIA, 1977.* Hearings before the Subcommittee on Health and Scientific Research of the Committee on Human Resources. United States Senate. 95th Congress. First Session on S. 1893. September 20 and 21, 1977; and *Biological Testing Involving Human Subjects by the Department of Defense, 1977.* Hearings before the above Subcommittee, March 8 and May 23, 1977. Senator Edward Kennedy was the Chair of both these sessions.

43.   *Human Drug Testing by the CIA*, 1977, p. 39.

44.   *Military Biology and Biological Warfare Agents. TM 3-216* and cross listed with *Air Force Manual 355.6*, Departments of the Army and Air Force, (Washington: 11 January 1956), Ch. I, paragraph 5.

45.   "The Status of Biological Warfare in International Law," *Military Law Review* (April, 1964), p. 89.

46.   Oppenheim, *International Law*, Vol. II, pp. 347-348.

47.   *Ibid.*, pp. 349-350.

48.   Cited in "Report on Human Rights in Armed Conflicts," United Nations (November 20, 1969). Report of the Secretary-General, A/7720.

49.   Captain Fred Bright Jr., "Nuclear Weapons as a Lawful Means," *Military Law Review* (October, 1965), p. 34.

50.   William V. O'Brien, "Some Problems of the Law of War in Limited Nuclear Warfare," *Military Law Review* (October, 1961).

51.   *The Law of Land Warfare* (1956), Section II, paragraph 34.

52.   Hanson W. Baldwin, *The Atlantic Monthly* (May, 1959), p. 37.

53. *Bulletin of the Atomic Scientists* (April, 1979), p. 20.

54. *Radiological Defense*, Vol. II. "The Principles of Military Defense Against Atomic Weapons." Armed Forces Special Weapons Project (November, 1951). Ch. 13, Summary.

55. Richard A. Falk, "The Shimoda Case: A Legal Appraisal of the Atomic Attacks upon Hiroshima and Nagasaki," *American Journal of International Law* (October, 1965), p. 759f.

56. *Ibid.*, p. 776.

57. *The Law of Land Warfare*, paragraph 35.

58. Cited in Falk, "The Shimoda Case," pp. 791-792.

Chapter 6
PROSECUTION
FOR WAR CRIMES IN HISTORY

Before there could be crimes of war there had to be laws of war. Before there could be laws of war there had to be customs of war. Before there could be customs of war there needed to be some sense that war had limits. The formal prosecution of the vanquished for supposed crimes of war did not arise at least until the Middle Ages when the Church Councils assumed the role of judge. These same Councils had also specified the offenses of war and the prescribed punishments. The more informal punishment of the vanquished by the victors was familiar in ancient times. Following the destruction of the Athenian fleet in 405 B.C. Lysander, the Spartan naval commander, called a meeting to determine the fate of the prisoners who had been accused of offenses against traditions of war. In his judgment, every person, with the exception of Adeimantus, was condemned to death. Adeimantus was spared because it was believed that he had opposed the plans to commit the purported brutalities. There was, however, no formal trial, nor were the rules the Athenians were accused of breaking clear. Every person found outside the city of Athens before the attack was executed and denied formal burial.

The emergence of the Holy Roman Empire supplied the "objective" judging body. St. Ambrose and St. Augustine had discussed the nature of just wars and had introduced at least the idea of proportionality between ends and means. In the official Councils of the Roman Catholic Church, philosopher, theologian, and politician seemed united under one body, and the Councils served as a more or less objective court for the prosecution of offenses of war. These Councils named the offenses and prescribed the punishments. Obviously their authority did not extend to non-Christians. During the years of their greatest influence, these Councils exercised sufficient power to carry out the proper sanctions. At the Council of Nicaea in 325, it was provided that Christians who, after their conversion laid aside their military trappings, but later returned to the military profession, would be charged with thirteen years of penance.[1] The criminality in this case consisted of being in the army as a Christian, rather than of using some offensive strategy or weapon. The offense was ecclesiastical. This same sacerdotal offense was expressed at the Council of Chalcedon in 451. In this instance those who returned to the military life after conversion to Christianity would be anathematized.[2] This judgment was reaffirmed in the canonical judgments of the Synod of Angiers in 453, Canon 7, and by the Synod of Tours in 461.

A clearer instance of a trial for breaking a law of war as opposed to a religious prohibition appeared at the time of the first Peace of God at the Synod of Charroux in 989. While the offenses were considered as religious sins rather than moral vice, the limits beyond which war makers ought not to go were emphasized. The limits in question concerned those persons who ought not to be slain. Protected persons had the status of innocents. For example, anyone killing or injuring a clergyman, priest, or deacon, who was not bearing arms or dressed in military garb, would be excommunicated.[3] It was evident from the Canon that clergy occasionally fought as soldiers, and that when they were in that role they were fair game for killing. In a new Peace of God announced by Guy of Anjou, Bishop of Puy, in 990 a form of the doctrine of military necessity appeared. The following prohibitions were listed, and every case, save one, included the qualification "unless," which prescribed a form of clerical necessity.

- No person in a bishopric shall break into a church, unless it is for the collection of taxes for the bishop.

- No clergy shall bear arms, and no unarmed persons accompanying clergy shall be harmed, unless such force is needed by a bishop or archdeacon in the effort to collect taxes.

- No person in the bishopric shall seize livestock, unless he requires them for a lawful expedition.

- No one shall seize peasants, men or women, with the intent to make them pay for their freedom, unless the peasant has already forfeited his freedom, or where the lord is dealing with his own serfs.

- No one shall seize church lands, unless by the order of a bishop.

- No one shall seize or rob merchants.[4]

o   No one shall seize or rob merchants.

The emphasis, in each case, was upon the notion of protected persons or places, unless there was some clerical (military) necessity. It was not clear why merchants should not be harassed even if some clerical advantage existed for doing so.

The idea of rules of war was extended in the Truce of God made for the Archbishop of Arles in 1035-1041 to cover those times when war was permissible. It was decreed that no fighting should occur during holy seasons between Wednesday vespers until sunrise Monday, leaving a rather short time for warmaking. Offenders would be excommunicated. If a soldier slew another on a truce day, he would be exiled to Jerusalem, apparently a kind of clerical Siberia. This was the secular part of the punishment. If the offender was also a Catholic, he would need to make a pilgrimage out of his Jerusalem stay. The Truce written for the Bishoprics of Besancon and Vienne in 1041 added even further days when fighting was prohibited. The Truce of the Bishopric of Terouanne prescribed exile of thirty years plus compensation to the injured parties for fighting on the wrong days. In 1103 Henry IV issued a Peace for the land of Maintz. The signators agreed not to attack either the person or the property of clergy, merchants, women, and Jews.[5] The punishments were proportional to the gravity of the offense, and ranged from loss of hair, beating with rods, to the loss of a hand or an eye.

At subsequent Councils the offenses were extended to cover both weapons and strategies. Incendiarism, the use of the crossbow or of poisons were declared criminal, especially if used against Christians. These prohibitions arose out the emergence of the military, knightly, religious tradition, which entailed a sense of sportsmanship. This one complex tradition stressed obedience to orders coupled with the belief that the soldiers who obeyed were free from censure. The rules by which soldiers were judged were clearly inapplicable to civilian life. Most of what soldiers did in battle was forbidden outside of battle. Thus if war was to be tolerated at all, then rules seemed in order. Like knightly jousts, the actions of soldiers were not to be carried out on city streets by everyone. An official field of battle, and formal rules for conduct existed. No great humanitarian sentiment was involved, since the nobility with which knights treated each other was not matched by any such concern where knights dealt with commoners or Saracens.

In the trial of Sir Peter Hagenbach in 1474, he was accused of having instituted a reign of terror in the town of Breisach. The charge against him was that he had instituted this terror without first having declared war. Had he declared war the acts would have been proper. Thus the declaration of war brought the rules of war into play as well as being a rule of war itself. Once war had been declared rules took effect. For example, the signal that a war of "no quarter" would be conducted was the raising of a red banner, and under it the enemy knew that no prisoners would be taken. "No quarter" was not, at that time, a crime, but to wage a war of no quarter without having first raised the red banner was a war crime. In the case of public or "open war" the sign was the unfurling of the banner of the prince. When this had been done, the soldiers could take spoil and enslave captives. Once the prince had unfurled his banner, his troops could not retreat. In war under the pennons, soldiers could kill and wound, but they could not burn or take spoil. In war to the death every man, woman, and child could be slain. In the case of cities which had refused to surrender when surrender had been demanded, the women occupants could be raped.[6] Each warring group had its own banners and pennons and any deception in their use was an offense of war. This rule appeared as a prohibition against perfidy in *General Orders 100*, paragraph 114; in *Rules of Land Warfare*, 1914, paragraph 192; in *Rules of Land Warfare*, 1934 , paragraphs 39-45, in the 1940 edition, paragraphs 39-44; and in the current *The Law of Land Warfare*, paragraph 50. Interestingly enough, the interpretation of perfidy became both vaguer and more restricted in each succeeding manual.

Even the practice of incendiarism, which had been condemned by Church Councils throughout the Middle Ages, could be excused as long as a formal declaration of war had been made. Indeed, once war had been declared virtually every act became permissible under superior orders. Raymond of Penaforte expressed the prevailing opinion that while incendiarism was prohibited, it ceased to be so if practiced in response to superior orders. The act was not even called incendiarism unless done without superior orders. Under the Roman Church Councils some precedent existed for believing there were crimes of war and for the conduct of trials to handle offenders.

EARLY U.S. WAR TRIALS

The trial of Captain Henry Wirtz, the commandant of the Confederate prisoner of war camp at Andersonville, Georgia was clearly a war crimes trial. The trial used *General Orders 100*, Article 59, as the basis for the charge against Captain Wirtz. Officers of the armies of the Union and the Confederacy had received copies of this Army manual. In addition, the first International Red Cross Conference had been held at Geneva in 1864, dealing primarily with the treatment of prisoners of war. Article 59, of *General Orders 100*, ruled that prisoners of war were answerable for war crimes committed before their capture. Wirtz was at the time a prisoner of the North. He was a Swiss medical doctor in charge of the camp at Andersonville. He pled superior orders and argued that the offenses had been the responsibility of those who set up the camp. He came to Andersonville after the camp had been established and had nothing to do with the conditions which he inherited. In spite of this he was sentenced to death. Considerable evidence showed that he had done his best under abysmal conditions for which he was not responsible. But the public mood after a long and bloody war needed a scapegoat.[7]

The American Army tried some of its own soldiers for alleged atrocities committed by them during the Philippine War of 1899-1902. After the trials, a civilian commission, headed by Charles Francis Adams, confirmed the judgments of the military tribunals. Brigadier-General Jacob H. Smith, U.S. Army, was tried April 24-May 3, 1902 for having given orders to Major L.W.T.Waller of the Marine Corps to take no prisoners on the island of Samar, Philippine Islands. When Major Waller had asked whether he was to kill every person capable of bearing arms, he said that the General had replied affirmatively. When the Major asked if there was a lower age limit, the General stated that ten years was the lower limit. The official charge against the General was "conduct to the prejudice of good order and military discipline."[8] While the court martial found General Smith guilty as charged, and it initially recommended that he be retired, the final sentence was limited to an admonishment.[9]

Major Edward Glenn of the Fifth U.S. Infantry was tried May 23-29, 1902 for having used torture to get information from one of the leaders of the insurrection, Tobeniano Ealdama. The form used was the "water cure," in which large quantities of water were forced into the stomach through the mouth. The Court denied the appeal to military necessity, and Major Glenn was found guilty. *General Orders 100*, paragraphs 56 and 75 forbade such treatment of prisoners, and it provided the basis for the trial. The sentence for Major Glenn, however, was merely suspension from command for one month and the forfeiture of fifty dollars in pay.[10] Lieutenant Preston Brown of the Second U.S. Infantry was tried June, 1901 for shooting a prisoner of war for having attempted to escape. The Lieber Code (*General Orders 100*), paragraph 77, had stipulated that while a prisoner may be shot while trying to escape, he may not be punished after his capture for having tried. Lieutenant Brown was tried for this violation. The Court found him guilty as charged and initially sentenced him with dismissal from the service and five years imprisonment at hard labor. This was reduced by President Roosevelt to forfeiture of half pay for nine months and a reduction in line ranking as a lieutenant.[11] In November,

1902 reports reached the Judge-Advocate-General's office that Captain Cornelius M. Brownell had applied the "water cure" to a Catholic priest, Augustine de la Pena, under which the priest died. While the facts were certified as true, the judge ruled that since Brownell was no longer in the military, he could not be tried. Furthermore, an act of June 6, 1900 had ruled that extradition of a person who had committed a crime held only if the crime was in a foreign country. Since the Philippine Islands was not considered a foreign country, extradition was not possible.[12]

At the close of World War I the Allies had appointed a "Commission on the Responsibility of the Authors of the War and on Enforcement Penalties." Its function was to investigate war crimes and to recommend appropriate action. The Commission made its report to the Preliminary Peace Conference in Paris, and recommended that the following acts should be prosecuted as crimes: "(a) Acts which provoked the world war and accompanied its inception; (b) Violations of the laws and customs of war and the laws of humanity."[13] The Commission recommended that the offenders, regardless of rank or authority, would be liable to prosecution. A High Tribunal was proposed to consist of three members from each of the five major Allied powers, and one each from the other Allied nations. While a majority of the Allies endorsed the recommendations of the Commission, the American representatives objected to the procedure for establishing the court on the premise that such a court had no precedent in international law.[14] The Americans, furthermore, refused to accept the doctrine of indirect responsibility as it applied to the high officials in government, nor would they accept the concept of negative criminality whereby a person could be prosecuted for having failed to prevent some criminal action. Finally, the American delegates rejected the thesis that heads of state could be tried. The trials proceeded, thus, without U.S. support.

The report of the Commission influenced the Treaty of Versailles. Article 227 of that Treaty provided that the German Kaiser Wilhelm II should be brought before the Court for offenses against international morality and the sacredness of treaties. Other high-ranking German officials were also cited, including the Kaiser's son, the Chancellor's grandson, and Marshalls von Hindenburg and Ludendorf. On February 3, 1920 a list of 896 alleged war criminals was submitted to Baron von Lersner, the German legate. He refused to accept the list, whereupon it was sent directly to the German government on February 7, 1920. The German Cabinet, however, refused to turn over the offenders, arguing that the war would be renewed should they do so. The Allies finally consented to allow the Supreme Court of the Reich of Leipzig to try the cases. This Court received a shorter list of 45 names, of which they agreed to try 12. Only four were found guilty. Karl Heynen, a non-commissioned officer in charge of a British prisoner of war camp in Westphalia, was found guilty of beating prisoners who tried to escape or who refused to work in the coal mines. He was sentenced to ten months in prison. Captain Emil Mueller, in charge of a prisoner of war camp at Flazy-le-Martel, was found guilty of brutality and sentenced to six months in prison. Private Robert Neumann was convicted of assaulting prisoners. The German submarine commanders were excused on the basis of superior orders. Major Benno Crusius was found guilty of shooting wounded French prisoners, and he was sentenced to two years. Five others were accused of atrocities against Belgian and French citizens, but they were acquitted. The Allies were dismayed at the light sentences, and the Allied Commission of Observers at Leipzig withdrew in protest. It was finally recommended in January 14, 1922 that no more cases be submitted to the Leipzig Court and that the Allies conduct the trials themselves following the provisions of Articles 228-230 of the Versailles Treaty. A few trials were held in Belgium and France before the idea was dropped.

Several obstacles hindered the Leipzig Trials from the start, quite apart from the unwillingness of the German Courts. In the first place, many Allies, including the United States, doubted that anyone could be tried for a war crime unless his own country first named the act a crime. In the second place, international custom prescribed that the soldiers had to be tried by courts in their own country and in accordance with the military code of that country. The presence of Allied judges contradicted this. The German Courts denied that their soldiers had been ordered to commit any illegal acts, and many Americans sympathized with the Germans on this score. Finally, it was asserted that no prior laws prescribed either the offenses charged or the penalties for having committed them. By any ordinary interpretation of international law both of these were required.

THE NUREMBERG TRIALS

American reticence and British enthusiasm at the time of the Leipzig trials was reversed during World War II by British reticence and American enthusiasm at the prospect of trials following that war. In order to avoid a repetition of what had happened at Leipzig, changes needed to be made on the score of who conducted the trials. To resolve this matter the Allies took the position that at the close of the war, no German or Japanese government existed and that, as a consequence, the victorious Allies constituted the official German and Japanese governments. Thus the Allies could, in accordance with international custom, organize the courts and conduct the trials. A further step was taken by the U.S. in altering the blanket protection soldiers had formerly enjoyed when following superior orders. The Allies stated, further, that both Versailles and the League of Nations had set some precedent. A most important requirement to allow the trials to take place was to identify the antecedent "laws of war" or "laws of humanity" which the Axis persons were said to have violated. The laws claimed to have been violated and the punishments for such violations clearly needed to have antedated the deeds in question. The laws of war, the breaking of which constituted war crimes, were rooted by the Nuremberg Charter in declarations of The Hague of 1899 and 1907. The laws of humanity, the breaking of which constituted crimes against humanity, were believed to have been established by conventions issued at Geneva Red Cross Conferences. The crimes against the peace were believed to have been stated in the Paris Peace Pact of 1928.

In January, 1943 some of the occupied nations joined in issuing the St. James Declaration which proposed that those guilty of such crimes should be punished through some channel of justice. George Manner, an international jurist, spoke for many of the international legal authorities when he raised doubt whether the St. James Declaration rested on any established traditions, and whether conducting such trials would entail making new rules after the fact.[15] His examination of the international laws then in force persuaded him that criminal acts of war would first have to constitute offenses within the municipality in which the offenses were committed before they could properly be considered to be war crimes. He noted, further, that "individuals are not subjects of the international law of war.... This rule is axiomatic in the law of war."[16] If this were true, then only states could be prosecuted and the result would be comparable to prosecuting a corporation, for which capital punishment would make no sense. The Allies issued the Moscow Declaration on October 30, 1943. It made the principal points that the Germans would be tried in those nations where their crimes were committed, while those whose crimes had no specific locale, would be tried by a procedure to be established later.[17] This occurred the following year in July, 1944 when the United Nations War Crimes Commission was established to gather evidence of war crimes. At this time the positions of the U.S. and Great Britain were reversed from what they had been during the Leipzig trials. The U.S. now wished to prosecute the German and Japanese Cabinet leaders, while the British opposed this plan. Viscount Simon feared that such trials would be simply propaganda which would be used against the Allies in the trials. The Viscount preferred to act as if the Axis leaders were outlaws and to have them shot on sight, even though they might have voluntarily surrendered. The Soviet Union agreed with the United

States and the two countries persuaded the British to join them in the conduct of the trials.

Between June 26 and August 8, 1945 the United States, the United Kingdom, the U.S.S.R., and France met in London to formulate the principles on the basis of which the trials would be conducted. Some fundamental differences existed among the four nations on matters of legal process. The Soviet tradition allowed courts to try cases without the parties being represented which was not the case in the U.S. and Great Britain. The U.S. wanted to include "aggression" and "conspiracy" as crimes. They were virtually alone in this wish. Only at the last minute did the Soviet Union agree to prosecute non-Nazis. Anglo-American law allowed the accused to speak in their own defense. Continental law allowed the defendant to make a final unsworn statement not subject to cross examination. This was resolved by allowing the defendants both options.

On August 8, 1945 an agreement was reached among the United States, Great Britain and Northern Ireland, France, and the U.S.S.R. for the prosecution and punishment of the major war criminals whose crimes had no specific location. Following the trials of this first group of Germans, would be further trials under the aegis of Control Council Law No. 10 in the specific countries where alleged offenses were charged. There would also be an initial Tokyo Trial of the leaders whose crimes had no specific locale, to be followed by trials of those whose crimes were in a specific place. The first International Military Tribunal was composed of four members, each with an alternate. In the event of illness or death of one or more of the judges, the trials could proceed without delay. Conviction required at least three affirmative votes. This Tribunal was to remain in session for a period of one year.

Article VI of the Charter of the International Military Tribunal stated the crimes for which the accused would be tried. They were:

o   Crimes Against the Peace. These included planning and waging an aggressive war as well as the conspiracy to do so.

o   War Crimes. These were violations of rules of war and emphasized maltreatment of prisoners of war, of civilians in occupied countries, and "devastation not justified by military necessity."[18]

o   Crimes against humanity. The emphasis was upon treatment of civilians, especially where the attempt had been made to exterminate a group on religious, political, or racial grounds. Article VI affirmed that the principal leaders of state were not exempt. Article VIII stated that obedience to superior orders would not be an excuse, although the fact that an order had been given to a subordinate would be an extenuating circumstance and could mitigate a sentence. Article IX granted to the Tribunal the power to declare that the organizations or groups to which the accused belonged were criminal organizations.

The Tribunal invited any member of such organizations to apply to be heard. By April 26, 1946 the Tribunal had received 81,433 such applications, most of them coming from prisoner of war camps. Members of the Nazi SS accounted for 58,597 of these applications. Shortly the number reached 110,000. The Defense Counsel visited 80 prisoner of war camps and as a consequence decided to allow additional witnesses. The Commission began its hearings May 20, 1946, and had listened to 603 persons by June 13, when a second commission was set up. This one heard an additional 101 witnesses. Affidavits were taken from prospective witnesses, and when the arbitrarily set time limit had been reached on August 5, 1946, 313,213 had been received. This International Military Tribunal conducted the initial trial of 24 German defendants whose crimes had no specific locale. The charge of a "common conspiracy" emphasized the role of the Nazi Party, especially as it had glorified war, persecuted Jews, invaded territory, and collaborated with Italy and Japan. The "crimes against the peace" stressed the role of Germany in Poland, Yugoslavia, Greece, Belgium, the Netherlands, Luxembourg, Norway, Great Britain, and France. "War crimes" concentrated on the extermination camps that included the 1,550,000 persons killed at Maidanek, the 4,000,000 at Auschwitz, 700,000 at Lwow, 200,000 at Ganov, 135,000 at Smolensk, in addition to the 4,978.000 Soviet citizens who had been deported. The "crimes against humanity" repeated the charges under war crimes with special emphasis on the fate of the Jews. What made all of this so heinous to the Court was that these deaths had no justification based on military necessity. Some 5,700,000 Jews were slain without any military excuse. Justice Robert H. Jackson expressed the dominant view of the Court that, "history does not record a crime ever perpetrated against so many victims or one carried out with such calculated cruelty."[19] "Crimes against humanity" played a dominant role, and none of the 24 accused was sentenced capitally unless he had been found so guilty. The list of the names, the charges, and the sentences may be found in the appendix. Many of the problems faced by the judges will be summarized under the section as to whether the Nuremberg Trials set any precedent.

TRIALS UNDER CONTROL COUNCIL LAW NO. 10

The details for prosecuting those Germans whose offenses had taken place in a specific country were explained in *Control Council Law No. 10*, published December 20, 1945. Acting under the provisions of this Law the United States issued Military Government Ordinance No. 7. It provided for the new tribunals with three members and one alternate each. The Allies had divided the war zones among themselves for determining which Allied nation conducted the trial. Every member of a Tribunal in an American zone would be a civilian lawyer from the U.S. Twelve initial cases were conducted by the Americans. A total of 185 persons were indicted and of these 177 were actually tried. The sentences are listed in Appendix B. In addition to the 12 cases which were heard, there were 84 other war crimes trials, a majority of them prosecuted by either the British or Americans. The United Nations War Crimes Commission analyzed all 84 cases, as well as 5 of the first 12. For example, the British conducted the Essen Lynching Case in 1945;[20] the Zyklon B Case in 1946;[21] the Belsen Trial in 1945;[22] the Trial of General von Falkenhorst in 1946;[23] and the Trial of Kesselring in 1947.[24] The Australians conducted the Ohashi Trial in 1946;[25] the Netherlands conducted the Trial of Susuki Motisuki in 1948;[26] and the Trial of Willy Zuehlke in 1948;[27] the French conducted the Trial of Bauer, Schrameck, and Falten in 1945;[28] and the Trial of Franz Holstein and Others.[29] Poland conducted the Hoess Trial in 1947.[30]

No accurate report exists of the total number of trials conducted since World War II and based on the Nuremberg precedent. As late as January, 1961, West Germany averaged one such trial every three weeks.[31] On January 13, 1961 a Warsaw court sentenced an accused for crimes committed during the occupation. An Israeli court sentenced Eichmann in December, 1961. At Dachau, to mention only one such camp where trials were held, the U.S. military commission tried 1,672 accused and convicted 1,416 of them.[32] A legal historian of the time estimated that up to January, 1949,

> exclusive of hearings in Russia... there are 2,116 known military tribunal hearings conducted by the United States, Great Britain, Australia, France, the Netherlands, Poland, Norway, Canada, China, and Greece. Of these the United States conducted 950 of which 500 were held in Europe and 450 in the Pacific theatre.[33]

War crimes were declared to have no statute of limitations by the U.N. General Assembly November 26, 1968. However, the vote of 58 yea, 7 nay, and 36 abstentions indicated very little support. Indeed, no

Western states, including members of the anti-Nazi coalition voted in favor. Only three Latin American states (Chile, Cuba, and Mexico) voted affirmatively. Objectors felt that such a convention would erode traditional human rights. It was, in addition, unclear how serious the offenses needed to have been before the statute should be waived. The vote did, however, give encouragement to Nazi hunters, and the Eichmann trial was a case in point.

THE TOKYO TRIALS

By a special proclamation of January 16, 1946 an International Tribunal for the Far East was established. The same charges were involved as had been the case at Nuremberg. The size of the tribunal was enlarged from the stated four at Nuremberg to not less than five nor more than nine. All members were appointed by General Douglas MacArthur, the Supreme Commander of the Allied Powers in the Far East. The members were selected from a list submitted by the signators of the Instrument of Surrender.[34] The panel was subsequently increased to eleven, consisting of one member from each of the following countries: Australia, Canada, China, France, Great Britain, India, the Netherlands, New Zealand, the Philippines, the U.S.S.R., and the United States. Like the Nuremberg precedent the first Tokyo Trial prosecuted those superior officers whose crimes had not been limited to any specific place and who could not plead superior orders. Twenty-five Japanese were tried, and the difference in severity of sentences between Tokyo and Nuremberg may be seen in Appendix C.

Considerable disagreement arose among the counsels of the Military Tribunal of the Far East. In view of the magnitude of this disagreement, Bruce Blakeney, on behalf of the entire defense counsel, filed a Defense Appeal to General MacArthur, charging that the trials had been unfair. His list included the following instances:

o   The prosecution did not present its case fairly.

o   The defendants did not receive a fair trial. Even the Chief Prosecutor admitted that some innocent persons were charged.

o   The Tribunal used two sets of rules: one for the prosecution and the other for the defense. The prosecution, for example, was permitted to use rumor, hearsay, and newspaper reports as evidence. Justices Pal of India, Bernard of France, and Roling of the Netherlands all underscored these malpractices.

o   Even the President of the Tribunal expressed serious
    doubts whether aggressive war was a crime and whether
    the Paris Pact had ever meant to establish it so.

o   The great mass of evidence from defense witnesses was
    never taken into consideration.

o   In no case did the bare seven-judge majority agree on a
    sentence. Death was voted with as few as four votes out
    of the eleven in support.

o   Unlike the Nuremberg Trials, where guilt or innocence was
    declared individually, at the Tokyo Trials it was declared
    en masse.

o   Men who had been outspoken against the militarism of
    Japan and also against its aggression were sentenced along
    with established aggressors.[35]

As in the case of the Nuremberg Trials the first Tokyo Trials
were followed by additional ones of persons whose crimes had been
located in a specific country. For example, the United States prosecuted
General Tomoyuki Yamashita before a military commission in the
Philippines and found him guilty of failing to control the operations of
his troops and permitting them to commit atrocities against civilians
and prisoners of war.[36] The U.S. Supreme Court noted in its opinion:

> The question then is whether the law of war imposes on an
> army commander a duty to take such appropriate measures
> as are within his power to control the troops under his
> command for the prevention of the specified acts which are
> violations of the law of war... and whether he may be
> charged with personal responsibility for his failure.[37]

The Court ruled in the affirmative, and General Yamashita was tried
and found guilty. Sufficient evidence, however, existed to establish that
Yamashita was far less responsible because of his distance from the
events than comparable officers, say, in the Son My or My Lai
massacres.

The British tried Gozawa Sadaichi and nine others in a British
Court in Singapore. The Right Honorable Earl Mountbatten noted that
only the accused whose sentences were likely to exceed seven years
would be tried. "War crimes" were defined in a Royal Warrant dated
June 14, 1945:

meaning a violation of the laws and usages of war committed
during any war in which His Majesty has been or may be
engaged at any time since 2nd September, 1939.[38]

The British had maintained at Nuremberg that only war crimes were
proper charges, and that crimes against the peace and crimes against
humanity had no precedent in law. In the British verdicts one defendant, Sergeant-Major Ono Tadasu, was acquitted; Kaniyuki Nakamure
was sentenced to be hanged; Gozawa Sadaichi was sentenced to twelve
years in prison; Chiba Masami was sentenced to seven years in prison;
Osaki Makoto and Ashiya Tamotsu were sentenced to five years in
prison; Tanno Shozo and Yabi Jinichiro to three years; and Okusawa
Ken was sentenced to two years.

On December 28, 1949 a Military Tribunal of the U.S.S.R. tried
twelve former Japanese servicemen and charged them with manufacturing and employing bacteriological weapons. Among the specific
charges was that a military expedition of the Japanese in 1940 was sent
to the Chinese region of Nimpo supplied with the germs of typhoid
and cholera and a large quantity of plague-infected fleas. As a result
of their use a plague epidemic had broken out. A similar expedition
had been sent to the region of Changteh in 1941 where plague also
erupted. In 1942 typhoid, paratyphoid, and plague-infected fleas were
used in central China. The Russian Tribunal decreed: a twenty-five year
prison sentence to Yamada Otozoo, Kajitsuka Ryuji, Takahashi
Takaatsu, and Kawashima Kiyoshi; twenty-year terms to Karasawa
Tomio and Sat Shunji; eighteen years for Nishi Toshihide; fifteen years
to Mitomo Kazuo; twelve years for Onoue Masao; ten years to
Hirazakura Zenzaku; three years for Kuroshima Yuji; and a two-year
term for Kikuchi Norimitsu.[39]

The Tokyo Trials, apart from satisfying an eye for eye retributive
justice, proved, for the most part, to be a source of legal embarrassment. The important question remaining after all the trials was whether
they established any precedent. Were we nearer to an international
consensus that crimes against the peace, crimes against humanity, and
war crimes did exist? The answers to these crucial questions will
revolve around conflicts between military traditions or rules and the
conventions of the international peace congresses like The Hague,
Geneva, and the United Nations. Further answers depend on whether
international jurists support the existence of laws of war and of
humanity. The consequences of using the most conventional weapons of
modern war now seem indistinguishable from what Germans and
Japanese were charged with doing, and a widespread fear has been
expressed that soldiers of any army might face prosecution for doing
their conventional duty. Let us turn now to these perplexing matters.

NOTES

1. H.J. Schroeder (ed.), *Disciplinary Decrees of the General Councils* (London: Herder, 1937), p. 41.

2. *Ibid.*, p. 96.

3. Oliver Thatcher and Edgar H. Neal, *A Sourcebook for Medieval History* (New York: Charles Scribner's), p. 412.

4. *Ibid.*, p. 414.

5. *Ibid.*, p. 419.

6. Maurice Hugh Keen, *The Law of War In The Late Middle Ages* (London: Routledge and Kegan Paul, 1965), *passim*.

7. Lewis L. Laska and James M. Smith, "Hell and the Devil: Andersonville and the Trial of Captain Henry Wirtz, C.S.A. 1865," *Military Law Review* (1975).

8. Leon Friedman (ed.), *The Law of War* (New York: Random House, 1972), Vol. I, p. 800.

9. *Ibid.*, p. 813.

10. *Ibid.*, pp. 814-819.

11. *Ibid.*, pp. 820-829.

12. *Ibid.*, pp. 830-841.

13. *American Journal of International Law* (1920), p. 95.

14. Friedman (ed.), *The Law of War*. pp. 851-852.

15. George Manner, "The Legal Nature and Punishment of Criminal Acts of Violence Contrary to the Laws of War," *The American Journal of International Law*. Vol. 37 (July, 1943).

16. *Ibid.*, p. 407.

17. *U.S. Army Pamphlet 27-161-2, International Law*, Vol. II. Ch. VIII, I,b. Cf. also *Trials of War Criminals Before the Nuerenberg Tribunals under Control Council Law No. 10*, Vol. I, p. viii.

18. *Nuerenberg Tribunals*. Vol. I, pp. xi-xvi.

19. Robert H. Jackson, *The Case against the Nazi War Criminals* (New York: Alfred Knopf, 1946), p. 35.

20. *Law Reports of War Criminals*, Fifteen Volumes. His Majesty's Stationery Office (London, 1948), Vol. I.

21. *Ibid*.

22. *Ibid*., Vol. II.

23. *Ibid*., Vol. XI.

24. *Ibid*., Vol. VIII.

25. *Ibid*., Vol. V.

26. *Ibid*., Vol. XIII.

27. *Ibid*., Vol. XIV.

28. *Ibid*., Vol. VIII.

29. *Ibid*.

30. *Ibid*., Vol. VII.

31. *U.S. Army Pamphlet 27-161-2*. Vol. I, p. 235.

32. *Ibid*.

33. John Alan Appleman, *Military Tribunals and International Crimes* (Westport, Conn.: Greenwood Press, 1971), p. x.

34. According to Article II of the Instrument.

35. Richard H. Minear, *Victor's Justice: The Tokyo War Crimes Trials* (Princeton: Princeton University Press, 1971), pp. 204-208.

36. Excerpts from the Supreme Court opinion on the matter of Yamashita, cited in Erwin Knoll and Judith Nies McFadden, *War Crimes and the American Conscience* (New York: Holt, Rinehart, and Winston, 1970), p. 194.

37. *Ibid.*, pp. 194-195.

38. See Colin Sleeman (ed.), *Trial of Gozawa Sadaichi and Nine Others* (London: William Hodge and Company, 1948), p. xvi.

39. *Materials on the Trial of Former Servicemen of the Japanese Army Charged With Manufacturing and Employing Bacteriological Weapons* (Moscow: Foreign Language House, 1950), p. 534.

Chapter 7
DID NUREMBERG AND TOKYO SET PRECEDENTS?

One of the first visible effects of the Trials was in the revisions which appeared in the major manuals on international law. In the classic work by L. Oppenheim, the new editor, H. Lauterpacht, expressed great hope that precedent had been set. He referred to the judgments of the Tribunal as being "evidence of international law"[1] and as "principles of International Law applicable generally and not only as against defeated enemies." While recognizing that the Tribunal was only quasi-international, he urged nations to establish genuine international judicial organs. He noted, parenthetically, that the victorious Allies would have "added substantially to the stature of the Nuremberg Trial by agreeing to have their own nationals tried."[2] He cautioned, however, against interpreting the failure to do this as basically undermining the importance of the Trials. The dismal international scene prompted him to observe,"There is no guarantee that any international institution, or International Law as a whole, will survive the onslaught of lawlessness."[3]

Any assurance that international law had been enhanced by the Trials received a setback when the General Assembly of the United Nations refused to ratify a proposal of the U.N. Commission on the Codification of International Law to formulate principles derivable from the Nuremberg precedent. The General Assembly was only able to agree to have the report read. In 1954 the same Commission presented a report on the nature of aggressive war and of crimes against the peace, and again the General Assembly rejected it. Either Nuremberg no longer seemed persuasive or else the renewed demands of national sovereignty had made it clear that war could not be allowed to become a crime. Several basic reasons supported this sad conclusion. Part of the problem lay in the nature of the Nuremberg charges and the difficulty, given the nature of modern war, in admitting that laws of war or limits beyond which armies ought not to go existed. Part of the problem, legally, was in proving that laws existed, the breaking of which would constitute the crimes in question: crimes against the peace, war crimes, and crimes against humanity.

THE CRIME OF WAGING AGGRESSIVE WAR

The Nuremberg Court was hindered from the outset by the lack of any clear definition from the past of what an aggressive war would be like to distinguish it from a defensive war. Traditionally, the nation which fired the first shots was the aggressor. The right of preemptive or first-strike offensives made it clear that the initiator of a war would not perforce admit to being the aggressor. Indeed, long before the first Hague Congress, nations tended to dismiss even the need to declare that a war was being waged. With modern weapons nations could not militarily afford what now seemed a knightly nicety in informing the enemy that hostilities were about to commence, or in waiting until the enemy had fired the first shot. If nuclear weapons were used, the first bomb sent on its way could be the last bomb of the war. Being the first to attack, then, became a military necessity. The term "aggression" was a slippery one; it functioned more as an exhortation than as a definition.

Most nations would, at one time or another, be guilty of aggression if first-strike became the *sine qua non* of an act of aggression. In medieval times it may have been possible to determine who had fired the first shot or made the first attack. While the American press had made a tabloid issue of the "sneak" attack of the Japanese at Pearl Harbor, no military leader of any nation would have expected an enemy to give advance warning when surprise was such a military advantage. Common custom identified the aggressor as the nation which occupied the land of another. The U.S. was, on these terms, the obvious aggressor in the Vietnam War, as well as in the invasion of Grenada, Nicaragua, El Salvador, or Panama. Modern weapons made it essential to develop "first-strike capability." The language of American military strategists at the time of Vietnam made evident that aggression was no longer a derogatory term. Part of the traditional meaning of an aggressive war was that it was indiscriminate and ignored the normal protections which innocents were supposed to enjoy. But with modern weapons of war every nation was an aggressor in this regard. Aerial warfare was the clearest evidence of the erosion of the combatant-noncombatant distinction. Allies and Axis alike made deliberate war on the civilian populations in World War II. For this reason the Nuremberg and Tokyo Trials made no indictments for what air forces had done. To a lesser degree this was the case for offenses committed in submarine warfare. Neither airplanes nor submarines could comply with the minimal requirements of The Hague Conventions.

General Telford Taylor observed that the traditional meanings of aggressive war had been obstacles to military success, and, as in the past, the effort to establish limits gave way to the pressures of military necessity. He noted, "Rules of war that interfere significantly with military success do not remain enforceable."[4] The charge that aggressive war was a crime had generated rules that interfered significantly with military success, and no one knew this better than military tacticians. Indeed, the lawyers for the German defendants had strenuously pointed out at the time of the Trials,

> no sovereign power had made aggressive war a crime at the time the alleged criminal acts were committed, that no statute had defined aggressive war, that no penalty had been fixed for its commission, and no court had been created to try and punish offenders.[5]

The prosecution still argued that such a crime did exist and that the Paris Pact of August 27, 1928 had outlawed war altogether (both aggressive and defensive). The prosecution argued that the Paris Pact was binding on the sixty-three nations which had signed at the time of the outbreak of World War II. Study of the Pact, however, failed to support this claim. The Pact, for example, did not even mention the term "aggressive war," nor did it specify any punishment for nations which resorted to war. Although the Pact did assert that recourse to war was now to be abandoned by its signators, no one intended this to mean that sovereign nations had relinquished their right to rise militarily in their own defense, let alone in their national interest.[6] After all, the U.S. Army pamphlet 27-10, *Treaties Governing Land Warfare*, made no mention of the Paris Pact in its list of treaties to which the United States felt bound, nor did that pamphlet consider aggressive war a topic of concern.[7]

It proved difficult for the Nuremberg Court to evaluate the degree of involvement of the accused in the claimed acts of aggression. The Tribunal standard for making this assessment that an accused was guilty or innocent of such crimes against the peace was that,

> There first must be actual knowledge that an aggressive war is intended and that if launched it will be an aggressive war. But mere knowledge is not sufficient to make preparation even by high-ranking military officers in the war criminal. It requires in addition that the possessor of such knowledge, after he acquires it, shall be in a position to shape or influence the policy that brings about its initiation or its continuation after initiation.[8]

But nations always consider that they are responding to aggression rather than initiating it. We Americans can appreciate this in the light of public revelations concerning the warrant for the actions after the Bay of Pigs, the Gulf of Tonkin, or the bombing by the U.S. of North Vietnam. What nation ever admitted that it was waging a war of aggression?

The conclusions of the various Tribunals did not present a univocal pattern. Every defendant in the Tokyo Trial was convicted of having waged aggressive war, while only eight of the twenty-four defendants at Nuremberg were so convicted. Not even the directors of Farben and Krupp were found guilty of complicity, even though they had provided the arms which made the war possible. Although five diplomats and government ministers were found guilty, no military leader faced the charge. In a reappraisal of the Nuremberg Trials, Marion E. Lozier raised the question,

> Has the overall result been affirmatively to incorporate Nuremberg precedent and practice, or has the response been instead a negative one, manifesting itself through forces of reaction, correction and rejection?[9]

Lozier's paper noted that the con side far outweighed the pro side. Consider, for example, that the International Law Commission of the U.N. had disclaimed any intent to establish international law; that the Draft Code had met with little support from member nations; that the United States had subsequently not felt compelled to support the Genocide Convention. This, Lozier claimed, was because nations generally felt that the Trials were based on "premisses legally faulty and politically dangerous."[10] There was no precedent for the notion of crimes against the peace or of a crime of waging aggressive war. Indeed, had Nuremberg set a precedent on this issue, many occasions since would have called for the precedent to be applied: Vietnam, Korea, Tibet, Hungary, Afghanistan, South Africa, Nicaragua, the Suez. All of this led the author to predict that if a Third World War was waged no such Tribunal would be reconstituted no matter what offenses were committed.[11] This conclusion was echoed by other legal scholars.[12]

WAR CRIMES

The problems here were fewer than with any of the other charges. If rules of war exist at all, surely those rules could judge crimes of war. Such rules had been assumed to exist ever since *General Orders 100* in 1863. Yet, even the simplest Hague prohibitions had been qualified by the doctrine of military necessity. Equally important, nations which refused to endorse Hague restrictions were not held culpable for breaking them. Furthermore, in wars with non-signators nations which had signed were relieved of their obligations. What was not guaranteed by appeal to military necessity was supported by appeal to the requirement of obedience to superior military orders. This was the case even though the 1944 revision of *The Law of Land Warfare* had claimed that such appeal was not an automatic escape from charges of having committed a war crime. The Yamashita Trial exhibited some of these problems in the interpretation of superior orders. Yamashita had been accused of failing to be aware of what his subordinates were doing in the Philippines, though considerable evidence showed that he could not possibly have known what was happening.[13] The findings of the Peers Commission, which investigated My Lai and Son My, made clear that the American officers were far closer to the events in question than Yamashita had been in his case. Part of the problem in interpreting whether superior orders constituted a defense relevant to responsibility for war crimes depended on what standard military practice was. What were soldiers accustomed to doing? What were recruits trained to do in basic training? Obviously no recruit was taught when it was proper to disobey.

Proportionality was another matter which gave the Courts difficulty. Were troops trained to use minimum force or were they trained in line with Clausewitz to assume that maximum firepower as soon as possible was the proper military strategy? In the Trial of Wilhelm List and Others under Control Council Law No.10 proportionality was at issue. The Tribunal had ruled that for the Germans to have killed 50 to 100 Communists for every German soldier slain was disproportional. Yet the Tribunal left unanswered what the proper number might have been. The impression was, however, that some number would have been acceptable. This issue appeared again in the Trial of Franz Holstein. Here the Germans were accused of burning three farms for every German soldier slain by the residents, and one farm for every German who had been wounded. Was there a proper number of burned farms in each case? In the Trial of General Lanz in Greece, it was determined that he was guilty of having issued an excessive reprisal order to acts of sabotage to an underwater cable. Ten Greeks had been shot for each such act. The Court ruled that this was an excessive number. Presumably a proper number could have been found. These cases presumed that while the acts in question were not criminal, the number of the victims of such acts was.

The Courts were on firmer ground in their charges against the Germans and Japanese for their treatment of prisoners. This was especially so in the extermination camps and in the face of the biological and psychological experiments conducted on prisoners. Here the judgments spoke to the fact of the deeds and not merely to the number of them, although the numbers did play a significant psychological role. The extermination camps could not be defended on any appeal to military necessity, nor could the slaughter of prisoners. Shooting large numbers of soldiers in battle was one thing, but the systematic slaughter of prisoners was quite another. This was not like shooting hostages which had become a matter of military strategy. Such extermination camps, partly because they were kept more or less secret, did not even have the claim that they helped to destroy enemy morale, an argument the Americans used to defend obliteration bombing of civilian centers. Suppose, however, that the German lawyers had been able to show that the death camps did serve an important military function. Would these killings then have been absolved of being war crimes? What if the death camps had "saved many German lives," an argument used by President Truman to justify the bombings of Hiroshima and Nagasaki? Would the Nuremberg judges have exonerated the accused Germans? Probably not, since the judges appealed to both The Hague and Geneva declarations to the effect that prisoners were protected by international law from the slaughter entailed in war. No amount of maltreatment of prisoners would ever be proportional.

CRIMES AGAINST HUMANITY

Article VI of the Charter of the International Military Tribunal had established the definitions of the crimes for which the accused would be tried. In the case of crimes against humanity the Article explained the acts constituting this offense as,

> murder, extermination, enslavement, deportation, and other inhumane acts against any civilian populations, before or during war; or persecutions on political, racial, or religious grounds in execution of or in connection with any crime within the jurisdiction of the Tribunal, whether or not in violation of the domestic law of the country where perpetrated.[14]

Leaders of state were not exempt from these charges, nor would the plea of superior orders by itself be accepted as extenuating.

Two factors influenced the Tribunal to concentrate on war crimes rather than on crimes against humanity. In the first place, the British had found no laws relevant to the charge of crimes against humanity.In the second place, the legal traditions assumed that prior to a war no crimes could be associated with that enterprise, and this would exclude those prior crimes against humanity. The Court hesitated to introduce offenses which antedated 1939. Yet, in spite of this, Telford Taylor stated in his final summation,

> this law is not limited to offenses committed during war... it
> can no longer be said that violations of the law and customs
> of war are the only offenses recognized by common interna-
> tional law.[15]

In spite of the lack of any clear measure of proportionality the sheer
numbers of persons slain in camps prompted the charge of inhumanity.[16] Typical of what had happened in the Eastern bloc countries
were the 1,550,000 killed at Maidanek, 4,000,000 killed at Auschwitz,
700,000 at Lwow, 200,000 at Ganov, 135,000 at Smolensk, 122,000 at
Leningrad, 11,000 Polish officers shot while prisoners of war, and the
deportation of 4,978,000 Soviet citizens. In part it was an issue of
genocide, the singling out of a specific group for reasons of race,
religion, or politics to exterminate such, if possible. The Court took the
position that neither the right of reprisal nor military necessity justified
such an attempt.

But if those in prison ought not to have been the target of
violence, should it not also have followed that the obliteration bombing
of civilian centers ought not to have been sanctioned? The obvious
initial implication was that the Allied and Axis air forces should also
have been prosecuted for making deliberate war on civilians. Perhaps
the medieval doctrine of the "double effect" operated to save aerial
warfare from such an otherwise reasonable indictment. It was argued
that the bombardier did not intend to kill civilians, hence should not
be held responsible for the deaths he could not reasonably be expected
to avoid. Unless air warfare was to be banned altogether, some such
casuistry was required to save it from the blanket indictment of being
that branch of the military which specialized in crimes against humanity. Yet, in spite of any uneasiness as to whether crimes against
humanity existed this charge was the most frequent one levelled against
the first 24 Germans tried at Nuremberg (see Appendix A).

Even during the Trials serious misgivings had been expressed over
whether modern mega-weapons of war had not made the singling out
of war crimes or crimes against humanity impossible. Even so obvious
a crime as the maltreatment of prisoners in chemical and biological
experiments did not have official support in the United States. While
the Tribunal had insisted that military necessity could not justify such
experiments, the fact was that the Germans were not alone in the
practice. The CIA and the DOD performed medical experiments on
unwitting American citizens between 1942 and 1977. These were
revealed at the Hearings at the Subcommittee on Health and Scientific
Research in 1977 elsewhere noted. At the direction of CIA Director
Helms vital information was withheld from the Kennedy Committee and
much of it burned so that it was unavailable. The research had been

given cryptic acronymic titles sufficiently incomprehensible so that nature of the projects was concealed. These experiments on human subjects bore such mysterious titles as MK-ULTRA, MK-SEARCH, MK-OFTEN, and MK-CHICKWIT. They were all on unwitting subjects many of which were given LSD and simulating brain concussions. What had happened to the brave hope of Justice Robert Jackson that the Nuremberg Court did not intend to prosecute Germans for any crime for which they were unwilling to prosecute Allied soldiers or citizens?

The two Hague Congresses had proposed a ban on weapons which caused "unnecessary suffering" or "superfluous injury." All the U.S. Army manuals, in principle, had endorsed this concern. Part of the Nuremberg indictment against the extermination camps was based upon the manner of the killing, giving the impression, as The Hague had, that ways of killing existed that went beyond necessity. If lances with barbed tips or projectiles filled with glass were "excessive" and caused "unnecessary suffering," then how could we reconcile this with napalm, chemical warfare, flame throwers, fragmentation bombs, booby traps, or aerial bombing which could never discriminate soldiers from civilians. Indeed, during the Trials and continuing to the present the American Army Chemical Corps developed, produced, and stockpiled for use, germ (bacteriological) weapons. If the failure to protect the innocent was a charge at Nuremberg, then modern armies surely stand indicted on the same charge. If killing soldiers or civilians *hors de combat* in prison camps was a crime based on The Hague and Geneva conventions, surely soldiers who use modern indiscriminate weapons on civilians should be subject to the same charge.

NUCLEAR WEAPONS AND NUCLEAR STRATEGY

The development of nuclear and thermonuclear weapons and the new strategies which they entailed signalled the demise of efforts to raise the conscience of Americans on the crimes of war, and signified that even the idea of criminality in connection with war had ceased to exist. The historic concern which had played so important a role at Nuremberg had centered on the excesses or disproportionality of the German and Japanese military acts, especially as they were directed against non-combatants or soldiers *hors de combat*. The Hague and Geneva declarations had been firm, even if unclear, on this score. "Unnecessary suffering" and "superfluous injury" were simply unwarranted. Nuclear war, however, marked the implicit acceptance of the strategy of holding civilians hostage and using them by acts of terrorism in the goal of crushing the enemy morale. Even the stoutest defenders of the theory of nuclear deterrence were aware that not only were the enemy citizens held hostage, but American citizens were in equal hostage. Indeed, a nuclear outbreak would jeopardize people all over the world. No other weapon in the past had ever posed the paradoxical consequence that the possession of the weapon was as much a threat to the possessor as to its proposed victims. Friends and enemies alike were threatened by weapons we readied for use. When the United States was the sole possessor of nuclear weapons our leaders had argued that no nation without such bombs would ever threaten a nation with the bomb. The theory rested on what was euphemistically called the threat of "massive retaliation." The threat would be effective only if our enemies believed that we would not cringe from bringing about such a retaliation. When both the United States and the Soviet Union were in possession of these bombs the theory of deterrence was based on "mutual assured destruction." It was presumed that neither the U.S. nor the U.S.S.R. would be so callous as to initiate a conflict which would annihilate both countries equally. Yet, if it were true that no nation in its right mind would initiate the first exchange of nuclear bombs, then it made no sense to claim that either nation would be willing to continue such exchange in reprisal. The shallowness of the theories of deterrence was revealed when our own administration began to speak of winning a nuclear war. Obviously if such a war could be won, then the deterrence which the possession of the weapons was supposed to exhibit did not exist. Proponents of winning nuclear war were, in effect, denying that nuclear weapons deterred. By the time of the Carter administration the ideas of "first strike," "limited counterforce," and "limited nuclear war" had become part of conventional military strategy. Nuclear wars were now eminently thinkable, and with this thought the last vestiges of hope that any conscience had developed on the crimes of war or crimes against humanity seemed to have vanished.

Nuclear weapons gave the final sanction to making war primarily on civilian populations and abolished any meaning to the combatant-non-combatant distinction. Military strategists either had to change the definition of what war was all about or deny that such weapons were weapons of war at all. With nuclear weapons war had become suicide. Their scope exceeded any conceivable military target. There ceased to be any unfortified cities in the sense discussed by Geneva and The Hague. In view of this, the United Nations passed a Resolution on Nuclear Weapons, November 24, 1961. The initial declaration stated,

> The use of nuclear and thermonuclear weapons is contrary to the spirit, letter, and aims of the United Nations, and as such, a direct violation of the Charter of the United Nations.[17]

The General Assembly requested the Secretary-General to determine whether the member states would agree to a convention prohibiting these mega-weapons, but neither of the nuclear powers nor those hoping to become such showed support. Since the obliteration bombing during World War II of essentially civilian centers, both military and civilian leaders had become accustomed to carnage against the innocent. This made it unlikely that humane concern could be generated about these new weapons. In any event, the same callousness which had led to the acceptance of flame throwers, napalm, and bio-chemical warfare now led to the acceptance of these weapons of Armageddon. There were voices in protest. Victor F. Weisskopf, Director-General of the European Center of Nuclear Research, insisted, "the first use of nuclear weapons of any kind by any power in any future conflict would be a crime against humanity."[18] George Kennan speaking at Princeton University was convinced that,

> the weapon of indiscriminate mass destruction goes farther than anything the Christian can properly accept...the law of war did not yet permit the punishment of whole peoples as a means of blackmail against governments.[19]

Paul Ramsey added his voice to this indictment:

> Any weapon whose every use must be for the purpose of directly killing non-combatants as a means of attaining some good and incidently hitting some military target is a weapon whose every use would be wholly immoral.[20]

Nuclear war commits us to the willingness to cause the very kinds of offenses branded as heinous at Nuremberg. It cancels the conventional distinction between combatant and non-combatant. Those who use or intend to use such mega-weapons could not plead before some future Nuremberg that our slaughter of innocents was unintended, nor could we claim that our real or intended target was some military installation. This situation is not altered by any claim that we propose merely "limited nuclear war," as if these weapons were like conventional bombs only a bit bigger. Hanson Baldwin quoted Vice Admiral "Cat" Brown on the matter: "I would not recommend the use of any atomic weapons no matter how small, when both sides have the power to destroy the world."[21]

Hans Morgenthau, a staunch defender of power politics, still warned that, "the use of nuclear weapons even if at first on a limited scale, would unleash unmitigated disaster."[22] McGeorge Bundy summed up the matter:

We think this inescapable risk is now so clear that all plans for "limited" nuclear war and all proposed deployments based on this concept, are deeply divisive and weakening to the Alliance.[23]

If the Nuremberg and Tokyo Trials are thought to have set any precedent for limits to what is allowed in war, then the manufacture, stockpiling, and threat to use nuclear weapons constitute evidence against any such precedent. At the same time, few would wish to turn the clock back and declare that no war crimes or crimes against humanity had been committed during World War II.

LEGAL RESERVATIONS OF THE TRIALS

Uneasiness in legal circles over the Trials was worldwide. Writers like F.B.Schick,[24] Marion Lozier,[25] Alwyn W. Freeman,[26] and Erwin Knoll and Judith Nies McFadden,[27] had expressed strong reservations. Even Telford Taylor admitted that "no definitive precedent had been established."[28] The International Tribunal underemphasized crimes against humanity, while Control Council Law No. 10 emphasized them without establishing a precedent. Part of this was due to the more provincial nature of the Control Council courts which prevented them from appearing as precedent setting. Over against this general legal skepticism, Quincy Wright, an historian and sociologist of war, believed that the "procedure constituted a model for an international criminal tribunal."[29] Thomas Dodd was convinced that the court was "completely adequate."[30]

Many legal scholars believed that the Trials had no prior basis in international law. The offenses for which the Germans and Japanese were tried did not exist in law. Hans Erhard, for example, said that the only basis for the Tribunal was the agreement signed by the United States, the U.S.S.R., Great Britain, and France so that the Charter was antedated by the offenses it was supposed to indict.[31] In addition, he noted that the judges came solely from the victors. No neutral judges or judges of their peers were involved. In accordance with Article V of the *Nazi Conspiracy and Aggression*, which was the official opinion and judgment of the Office of the United States Chief Counsel for Prosecution of Axis Criminality, signatures of support from other countries were sought. In spite of all the publicity only nineteen governments of the United Nations signed in approval: Greece, Denmark, Yugoslavia, Netherlands, Czechoslovakia, Poland, Belgium, Ethiopia, Australia, Honduras, Norway, Panama, Luxembourg, Haiti, New Zealand, India, Venezuela, Uruguay, and Paraguay.[32]

In some instances the German lawyers persuaded Allied legal scholars. In both the Hostage Case and the List and Others Case the German lawyers were successful in arguing that these cases rested on premisses inconsistent with the customs of war. In particular, emphasis was put on the tradition requiring soldiers to obey the orders of their superiors. Custom was against finding individual soldiers culpable for following orders. Indeed, the German lawyers cited an 1840 case in which McLeod, a British subject had been arrested for sinking an American ship, the Caroline, in which an American citizen had lost his life. The British ambassador demanded the immediate release of McLeod since he had been following superior orders. The American Secretary of State, Daniel Webster, agreed with the ambassador.[33] In fact, at the start of World War II neither the *British Military Manual* nor the American Army *Rules of Land Warfare*, allowed for the punishment of soldiers who were obeying orders. While in the Hostage Case the Tribunal had rejected the appeal to superior orders as justifying the shooting of hostages, the British and American manuals allowed for such shooting where hostages had committed hostile acts.

Richard H. Minear shared the British view that only war crimes should properly be the basis for the Trials so that the stress of the Tribunals on crimes against humanity and crimes against the peace were without legal precedent. Minear saw five difficulties generated by the Tokyo Tribunals:

o   No precedent existed for conspiracy as a crime.

o   Tradition protected the individual soldier when following orders.

o   No precedent existed for claiming aggressive war was a crime.

o   Negative criminality was not part of war traditions.

o   The Tokyo Charter was *ex post facto*.

Justice Pal, one of the judges at the Tokyo Trials, denied that the attack of the Japanese on Pearl Harbor constituted a treacherous act since relations between the U.S. and Japan were not peaceful at the time.[34] It was a sad indictment of the status of international law and international sentiment that it proved so difficult to prosecute for the kinds of offenses in the extermination camps. It was also deplorable that conventional military practices so closely approximated many of the crimes named at Nuremberg that, with rare exception, the *tu quoque* accusation could be made to the judges of the accused.

Franz B. Schick was particularly bothered by the lack of any precedent for the crime against the peace. He had argued that this crime was the primary basis for the Trials. If crimes against the peace were a doubtful category then all the subsequent charges made by the Tribunal would collapse.[35] If neither the Germans nor the Japanese had fought a war of aggression, then the conventional customs of war would have protected them from most of the remaining charges. Schick discounted the Allied claim that the Allied Occupation Government was the official government of Germany, thus escaping the charge that the Tribunal was composed of foreigners. He also discounted the appeal of the Tribunal to the Paris Pact, the League of Nations Treaty of Mutual Assistance, the Preamble to the Geneva Protocol of 1925, the League of Nations General Assembly of September 24, 1927, and the Sixth Havana Pan-American Conference. None of these had ever been made law, nor did any of them accord with international military practice. He concluded, "individual criminal responsibility for illegal resort to war is, beyond doubt, no generally recognized rule of international law."[36]

Most of these legal reservations were summed up by August Von Knieriem, general counsel for I.G.Farben. Von Knieriem had himself been charged at Nuremberg but found innocent of all charges and acquitted. His book on the Trials summarized the predominant German position. He made the following points:

o Control Council Law No. 10 was based on *ex post facto* laws.

o Contrary to Allied claims, Control Council Law No. 10 contained new laws not found in past tradition: for example, that individuals could be prosecuted for following military orders.

o The Court violated existing international law to the effect that the trials should be conducted by the courts of the land where the offenses were committed and based on laws of that land.

o The Trials were based on Anglo-American legal procedure.[37]

Naval warfare, like aerial warfare, confronted the Tribunals with serious difficulties since both Axis and Allies were guilty of the traditional crimes named at The Hague and Geneva Conferences. Edwin Borchard noted that the U.S. Navy had abandoned the concept of neutrality during World War II.[38] In February, 1946, the American government announced that its submarines had sunk 1,944 Japanese merchant marine vessels and 276,000 civilian Japanese had drowned as a consequence. This was in violation of the London Treaty of 1930 as well as of The Hague Conventions of 1899 and 1907. Indeed, if the letter of those prohibitions had been adhered to, the U.S. could not have fired its new cruise missiles since they lacked accuracy sufficient for the user to know whether the passengers or crew of ships which they sank were cared for in accordance with Hague Conventions. Some writers concluded from this that both submarines and cruise missiles were simply illegal.[39]

The emergence since World War II of wars of liberation, guerrilla wars, vigilante brigades (commonly called terrorists), and wars fought by United Nations forces complicated the legal task of determining what, if any, precedent Nuremberg set for these kinds of fighting. The Middle Ages had some precedent for assuming that wars for ideology, between believing Christians and heathen, had no rules which needed to be followed. Many who fought wars of liberation saw their situation as did medieval inquisitors or crusaders. In their view one side was the bearer of virtue and the other the perpetrator of oppression. Surely, they argued, the side of evil was not entitled to be treated with the deference normally given to conventional soldiers. Enough international uneasiness existed on this score that Josef L. Kunz urged in 1956 that wars of liberation, insurrection, and the like should be bound by the same laws of war supposed for conventional wars.[40]

I.P. Trainin held that guerrilla forces should be covered by the conventional laws of war.[41] Lester Nurick and Roger W. Barrett believed, however, that some guerrillas did not satisfy the conditions of being soldiers. While it would be prudent to treat them as if they were covered by laws of war, Nurick and Barrett doubted this was required by law.[42] After all, many liberation or "terrorist" forces denied that their enemies deserved any protection under laws of war. Eugene A. Korovin, Professor of International Law at the University of Moscow Juridical Institute of the Ministry of Justice, believed that struggling national resistance groups ought not be required to abide by the strict rules of war due to their relative weakness. He queried,

> Can we confine a sacred people's war against an aggressor and enslaver... can we confine this war within the strict bounds of the Hague rules, which were calculated for a totally different international situation?[43]

In the light of this Jacques Freymond warned,

> The temptation to establish privileged categories of com-
> batants who are fighting for a cause regarded as the only just
> cause, or as being more just than the other, must be
> avoided.[44]

A special problem arose for United Nations forces. Were they like policemen or like soldiers? Were they bound by the same laws of war as national armies? Some, like Howard Taubenfeld, felt that laws of war in their conventional form are not *prima facie* binding on international forces.[45] But once an exception is made here, then little reason exists not to allow the same latitude for liberation forces who see themselves, like U.N. forces, as the bearers of truth and justice.

Would the Nuremberg Trials under Control Council Law No.10 continue indefinitely, or did a statute of limitations apply here? If such a limitation existed, then by 1952 any as yet untried criminals would be safe from prosecution. Did a body exist empowered to override this law? On November 26, 1968 the General Assembly of the United Nations approved a convention which ruled that crimes against humanity and war crimes had no time limit for their prosecution.The convention had little support with a vote of 58 yea to 7 nay and 36 abstentions. No Western states, including members of the anti-Nazi coalition signed, and only 3 Latin states voted affirmatively (Chile, Cuba, and Mexico). The objectors to the convention feared that it would erode traditional human rights. It was also unclear how serious the offense needed to have been before the statute ought to be waived. Nations could not be compelled to extradite such accused, although as in the Eichmann case, Nazi hunters might continue as best they could to carry out their search. Thus the era of the Nuremberg and Tokyo Trials had come officially to an end. Was this also the end of any hope that future war crimes trials might be held if needed? Were these Trials simply instances of victor's justice?

NOTES

1. L. Oppenheim, *International Law* (London: Longmans, 1952), Vol. II, paragraph 257.

2. *Ibid.*, paragraph 257b and footnote, p. 585.

3. *Ibid.*, paragraph 257b.

4. Erwin Knoll and Judith Nies McFadden (eds.), *War Crimes and the American Conscience* (New York: Holt, Rinehart and Winston, 1970), p. 9.

5. U.S. Army Pamphlet 27-161-2, *International Law*, Vol. II, p. 236.

6. F.B. Schick, "The Nuremberg Trial and the International Law of the Future," *The American Journal of International Law*, Vol. 41 (October, 1947).

7. Cf. Table of Contents of Pamphlet 27-10. Nor is there mention in the current *The Law of Land Warfare*, pp.4-5.

8. Pamphlet 27-10, *Treaties Governing Land Warfare*, p. 239.

9. Marion E. Lozier, "Nuremberg: A Reappraisal," *The Columbia Journal of Transnational Law*. Vol. I and II, p. 64.

10. *Ibid.*, p. 67.

11. *Ibid.*, p. 76.

12. Cf. Alwyn Freeman, "War Crimes by Enemy Nationals Administering Justice in Occupied Territory," *The American Journal of International Law*, Vol. 41 (July, 1947); and Schick, "The Nuremberg Trials."

13. Cf. Knoll and McFadden (eds.), *War Crimes*, pp. 194-195.

14. For the entire text of the Charter of the International Tribunal see, U.S. Army Pamphlet 27-161-2, *International Law*, Vol. II, pp. xi-xvi.

15. Telford Taylor, *Final Report to the Secretary of the Army on the Nuernberg War Crimes Trials under Control Council Law No. 10* (Nurenberg, 1949), pp. 224-226

16. Cf. *The Trial of Major War Criminals: Proceedings of the International Military Tribunal Sitting at Nuremberg* (Nuremberg), Pt. I. pp. 2-30.

17. Leon Friedman (ed.), *The Law of War* (New York: Random House, 1972).

18. Victor F. Weisskopf, "Nuclear War: Four Pressure Points," *Bulletin of the Atomic Scientists* (January, 1982), p. 2.

19. George F. Kennan, "Foreign Policy and Christian Conscience," *Atlantic* (May, 1959).

20. Paul Ramsey, *War and the Christian Conscience* (Durham, N.C.: Duke University Press, 1961), p. 162.

21. Hanson W. Baldwin, "Limited War," *Atlantic*, CCIII, No.5 (May, 1959).

22. Hans Morgenthau, *New Republic* (October 20, 1979).

23. McGeorge Bundy, "No First Use Needs Careful Study," *Bulletin of the Atomic Scientists* (June, 1982).

24. Schick, "The Nuremberg Trial," *The American Journal of International Law*.

25. Lozier, "Nuremberg."

26. Freeman, "War Crimes."

27. Knoll and McFadden, *War Crimes*.

28. Taylor, *Final Report*. p. 109.

29. Quincy Wright, "The Nuerenberg Trial," *Journal of Criminal Law and Criminology*. Vol. 37 (March, 1947), p. 478.

30. *Ibid.*, p. 360.

31. Hans Erhard, "The Nuremberg Trial Against the Major War Criminals and International Law," *The American Journal of International Law*. Vol. 43, No.2 (April, 1949), p. 225.

32. *Nazi Conspiracy and Aggression* (Washington: U.S. Government Printing Office, 1947)

33. *Trials of War Criminals Before the Nuernberg Military Tribunals under Control Council Law No. 10.* Vol. XI (Washington: U.S. Government Printing Office, 1949), pp. 859-860.

34. Richard H. Minear, *Victor's Justice: The Tokyo War Crimes Trials* (Princeton: Princeton University Press, 1971), p. 158.

35. Franz B. Schick, "Crimes Against the Peace," *The Journal of Criminal Law and Criminology*, Vol. 38, No. 5 (January-February, 1948).

36. *Ibid.*, p. 459.

37. August Von Knieriem, *The Nuremberg Trials* (Chicago: Regnery, 1959), pp. 187-189.

38. Edwin Borchard, "Editorial Comment: The Effect of War on Law," *The American Journal of International Law*, Vol. 40 (July, 1946).

39. D.P.O'Connell, "The Legality of the Naval Cruise Missiles," *The American Journal of International Law*, Vol. 66 (October, 1972).

40. Josef L. Kunz, "The Laws of War," *The American Journal of International Law*, Vol. 50 (April, 1956).

41. I.P.Trainin, "Questions of Guerrilla Warfare in the Law of War," *The American Journal of International Law*, Vol. 40 (July, 1946).

42. Lester Nurick and Roger W. Barrett, "Legality of Guerrilla Forces Under the Laws of War," *The American Journal of International Law*, Vol. 40 (July, 1946), p. 583.

43. Eugene A. Korovin, "The Second World War and International Law," *The American Journal of International Law*, Vol. 40 (October, 1946), p. 753.

44. Jacques Freymond, "Confronting Total War: A 'Global' Humanitarian Policy," *The American Journal of International Law*, Vol. 67 (October, 1973), p. 687.

45. Howard Taubenfeld, "International Armed Forces and the Rules of War," *The American Journal of International Law*. Vol. 45 (October, 1951), p. 676.

Chapter 8
WAR CRIMES
AND LAWS OF WAR

We have come to the close of what has been a very dismal story. On the one hand we wanted to be convinced that at least the extermination camps of the Nazis were undebatable offenses which no civilized person should have tolerated. Yet, we rejected the effort of the United Nations to confirm that Nuremberg set a precedent. We were significantly less confident of the criminality of bombing essentially civilian targets as in the cases of Dresden, Berlin, Tokyo, London, Hiroshima, and Nagasaki. We were troubled because bombing civilians was good military strategy, and we did not want a good strategy to be labelled criminal. We felt on safer grounds dealing with maltreatment of prisoners, but perhaps because it was not good military strategy in the first place and thus entailed needless killing. Indeed, at the time of the Nuremberg Trials the slaughter of prisoners seemed utterly barbarous and without any redeeming military justification. Furthermore, the systematic attempt to exterminate the Jewish people in what the Nazis called the "final solution" was intentional and not the consequence of the accidental killing of civilians when some other military object was the real target. The initial attack on the Jews antedated the outbreak of the war, and this suggested that it could not be a crime of war. It was not obvious that bombing from the air of innocent civilians was "better" than the face-to-face killing in the death camps, but at least bombardiers could not be accused *prima facie* of taking sadistic pleasure.

We noted at the outset that the identification of crimes against humanity and war crimes presupposed rules or laws of war. We noted how throughout the history of war human sensibilities were able to rise to accept every escalation of brutality which new military technology made possible. In spite of the immensely increased havoc which modern wars could inflict, the laws of war, such as they were, remained unchanged. We still deplored only lances with barbed tips and projectiles filled with glass. The former had been prohibited in the Middle Ages on the grounds that they caused unnecessary suffering. But at the same time that we assured ourselves that humanitarian limits existed beyond which we would not go, we accepted flamethrowers, napalm, gas, noxious chemicals, booby traps, and nuclear bombs. The escalation of violence now possible simply led to an escalation of tolerance, and no way appeared to speak of humanity and chivalry which made any sense. In spite of this, the current Army manual still states that the principle of military necessity is conditioned by the requirements of humanity and chivalry.[1] Have we come full circle so that we must now admit that we are all barbarians, that no laws of war and no humanitarian restraints exist and that we have no premises from which to salvage the kinds of moral judgments implicit in the Nuremberg and Tokyo Trials?

RELIGION AND WAR CRIMES

The Judeo-Christian traditions had always vacillated between the blanket rejection of involvement in any civic venture, including the military, and the wholesale acceptance of war as the proper domain of Caesar if not Jehovah. War was either rejected altogether or embraced with religious fervor. To be sure, St. Augustine had initiated concern with the relation between the means and ends of war, but he was a good citizen in the sense that participation in soldiering was no more of a problem than participation in politics. His analysis of the nature of a just war provided no moral reasons for rejecting war as a method, even though he suggested some checks against too many wars. While he claimed that the barbarians from the north waged wars with needless cruelty, he still allowed Christians to wage war which he had conjectured would be more humanely conducted. The Old Testament stories of battles sanctioned by Jehovah gave no basis for moral sensitivity from that source. The record in *Isaiah* 13:1-19 was a monstrous one of wholesale slaughter of men, women, and children, all done with the claimed blessing of God and true believers. Religious indifference to the sufferings in war was worldwide. War was an inevitable human activity. In spite of the anguish of Arjuna in the Bhagavad Gita, the conclusion of that religious tract was that war was a necessary, if tragic, part of the human condition. Nor was the New Testament any more sensitive to the public and organized killing of war. Christians were, initially, uninvolved, because they had no earthly kingdom, and when they got an earthly kingdom in the Roman empire, they hastened to protect it as zealously as had their Jewish forbearers.

To be sure, exceptions arose to this general endorsement of the secular enterprise. Tertullian, for example, claimed that being a soldier was inconsistent with being a Christian.[2] However, he saw war not as a humanitarian problem but one of conflicting loyalties. It wasn't so much that Christians would be asked to perform immoral acts as that they would have to perform heathen acts of impiety. The adjustment from the position of general non-involvement of early Christians to becoming active participants in the secular battles was initiated by the writings of St. Augustine. He was not a pacifist and expressed little interest in doing more than legitimizing war. Wars were to be declared by the proper authority, fought for ends that were just, and with intentions which aimed ultimately at peace. The analysis of these matters was left to secular authority.

Medieval church councils did initiate attempts to set limits to the means by which wars were waged. They identified the proper days for fighting and the proper targets of violence. They also identified improper weapons such as incendiaries, poison, and the crossbow. In spite of the theological baggage entailed in the penalties for infractions, these councils did provide the foundations for two important subsequent principles: a sense of proportionality and the combatant-non-combatant distinction. The former implied criteria for declaring some weapons disproportional, while the latter gave criteria for prohibiting some strategies as indiscriminate. At the time, however, these efforts ran counter to the prevailing presumption of the principle of military necessity. By the time of John of Salisbury in 1159 the military functioned as the arm of religion and the state and any notion of limits appeared lost.

Just war theorists had played into the hands of emergent national leaders. Once the role of the authority empowered to declare war was stressed, the same authority seemed to have the right to deal with any remaining questions of ends or means. Modern nations have not deviated from this assumption. Soldiers might be urged to kill with compassion but this simply meant that they did so with dispassion. By the time of Martin Luther it had been well established that "onward Christian soldiers" was no mere pious platitude. Yet, protests against this religious acceptance of the warrior's role did occur, particularly among Protestant leaders. Erasmus (1467-1536) rejected the idea that Christians could be soldiers, not only against other Christians but against infidels as well. He queried, "Is it not a monstrous thing if a Christian shall fight with a Christian?"[3] George Fox, the Quaker, turned down a captaincy in the Commonwealth army on the grounds that the way of Jesus prohibited holding such an office. He wrote in his *Journal* in 1659 that anyone who claimed to fight wars for Christ was mistaken.[4] Tolstoy had said that Christians should not be murderers in uniform.[5] Indeed, Christian denominations like Quakers, Shakers, Mennonites, and Russellites were established on the premise that absolute pacifism was the Christian obligation. Conscientious objection to war on Christian religious grounds in the United States goes back to the American Revolution, and pacifists were recognized as such in that war as well as in the Civil War, World Wars I and II, Vietnam, and Korea. The pacifist tradition, however, does not help us in efforts to set limits to war making, since that tradition rejects war altogether no matter what weapons are used. Nonetheless, what this tradition calls attention to are the very paradoxes implicit in the war enterprise with respect to the hope to "humanize" or set limits to how wars are waged. Pacifists had concluded that war was not capable of being reconciled with humane concerns. They were committed to the premise that a "humane way of killing" was a contradiction. But as far as religion generally was concerned no univocal position emerged and the appeal to religion to resolve our humane doubts will not suffice. Religious leaders during World War II illustrated the haziness of any supposed Christian message on the subject. Emil Brunner affirmed, on the one hand, that force was inimical to the Christian message but if Christians wished to be good citizens they had to conclude that divine love commanded them to kill for the state.

> A State which is not prepared to defend itself by force of arms might just as well hand itself over to a more virile State, which, as a conqueror, does not hesitate to use these violent methods. To deny on ethical grounds, this elementary right of the State to defend itself by war simply means to deny the existence of the State itself.[6]

John Bennett concluded that "it may be our duty to do that which morally repels us."[7] Reinhold Niebuhr believed that in an immoral society Christians must commit evil.[8] This is not very instructive unless these same writers can inform Christians which evils they are commanded to commit. Christians assisted in the extermination camps, particularly against the Jews. Was this one of those evils Christians were obligated to commit? Did Emil Brunner intend that we should not deny to any State whatsoever the right to war in its national interest? This may well be an immoral society, as Niebuhr so rightly insisted, but surely this does not entail that Christians have *carte blanche* in the immorality they feel called on to commit in response. If war crimes or crimes against humanity do exist, Christians need to be enlightened as to when immorality in defense of the State should not be sanctioned.

MILITARY TRADITIONS AND THE LAWS OF WAR

The first and foremost concern of the early jurists was rooted in a commitment to emerging sovereignties. War was a major way sovereign states kept their boundaries secure. Little likelihood existed that rules would ever be formulated, or accepted if they were formulated, which would require states to surrender or to put themselves at a disadvantage with respect to their neighbors. No matter what the cause, every nation claimed that it was justified in coming to its perceived defense. However, the traditions from knighthood were not easily dismissed, and the suspicion always remained that nominal rules of war existed. The jurists beginning with Victoria had assumed the rules existed, and within the limits imposed by the demands of military necessity, they did rather well in their efforts to identify the limits, even though they understood that virtually every limit could be surpassed under sufficient military urgency. Most national armies were willing to poison, plunder, slaughter women and children, and bomb unfortified places if to do so would be strategic. The jurists shared with the military the view that "the sovereign has the right to do to the enemy whatever is necessary to weaken him."[9] The principle of military necessity was never in jeopardy on grounds of humanitarian sentiment. The requirement of obedience guaranteed absence of debates on these issues in the armed service. Soldiers were not expected to evaluate the ends or means ordered by their leaders. Nor could anyone have expected the soldiers to evaluate the weapons they were told to use to determine if they caused unnecessary suffering or violated the much praised principles of humanity and chivalry.

Francis Lieber, the author of *General Orders 100* in 1863, had insisted that soldiers must remain moral persons. He insisted that limits existed, and he named some of them. The problem was that military necessity had to be accepted, the right of reprisal had to be admitted, and obedience to superior orders had to be conceded. Was there any way to reconcile these three doctrines with any sense of moral limits? It was no help for Lieber to urge that it should be forbidden to show bad faith, to be needlessly cruel, to use torture to exact information, to destroy wantonly, to commit perfidy, or to declare no quarter. The fact was that military doctrines allowed every act in a military extremity. Such extremities seemed to be the rule. Military necessity was never in jeopardy, since laws of war were written with the protection of military necessity in mind. As long as military leaders determined whether a weapon caused "unnecessary suffering," it was a foregone conclusion that no useful weapon would ever be banned. The Hague, Geneva, and United Nations efforts were defeated by this all-encompassing military doctrine. Wars of "no quarter" had been banned by the Army manuals since 1863, but modern weapons of war committed armies to wars of extermination. Soldiers were not supposed to cause "unnecessary suffering" and all the Army manuals endorsed this prohibition, but the weapons in our arsenals guaranteed that we would do exactly what The Hague, Geneva, and the United Nations had forbidden. Moderation was never a term in the Clausewitz vocabulary, and no U.S. Army manual up to the current one ever stated otherwise. Warriors had rules with respect to life in the military, but no room appeared for any morality concerning how they fought their wars. Should we ever expect that the CIA, the DOD, the Pentagon, the Army Chemical Corps, or the State Department would take a moral stance and ban one of their own new weapons on grounds of humanity? The United States has no "banned" weapons in its arsenals by its own insistence, though many of them have been on the prohibited lists of The Hague, Geneva, and United Nations. Nonetheless, the notion of "clean" and "unclean" ways of killing the enemy has persisted. This notion was the subject of correspondence between General Canrobert, the French commander, and General Osten-Sacken the Russian commander at the battle of Sebastapol, January, 1855:

> The former who was evidently of the mind of Sir Lucius O'Trigger that you should kill your man "decently and like a Christian," complained that hooked poles which the Russians occasionally used, though not forbidden by war law, were certainly not the arms of courtesy.[10]

If hooked poles are rarely used in the twentieth century, it has not been for reasons of Christian charity, but because they are less effective than bayonets and surely less so than an M1 rifle. No one expects soldiers to choose hooked poles when they have at their disposal napalm and fragmentation bombs.

From the point of view with which the soldier has been indoctrinated, moral reservations concerning the kind and amount of violence against the enemy will always be out of place. When commanded, soldiers do their patriotic duty. It makes no sense to issue lethal weapons, assure the bearer of those weapons that he may wound or kill the enemy with them, and yet insist that he worry about what he is doing. It should not be forgotten, in spite of this, that moments of kindness toward wounded enemies and the sharing of food with vanquished non-combatants has commonly existed side by side with the most callous disregard for how armed conflict is conducted. This treatment may be a carry over from the days of knighthood, it may reflect the belief that when armed battle is over, a new set of rules takes effect, or it may indicate that some men can never be completely brainwashed of their civilian sensibilities. It may illustrate that some human beings never quite lose their ordinary humanity, no matter what they are taught in boot camp. Soldiers of every army are expected to obey their commanders, salute their flags, honor their profession, and "love" their country. This has been the rule no matter what the politics or what the goal, and German, Russian, British, or American soldiers did not differ in these regards. To be sure, individual soldiers have risen differently to the demands of battle. Studies from the Korean War indicated that most soldiers fired their rifles into the air and were never willing to fire at another soldier.[11] Others, like some at My Lai and Son My fired indiscriminately at everything that moved.

A genuine contradiction occurs here and no helpful solution appears on the surface. No national leader can afford, nor justify, to send troops into battle with less than the most sophisticated and deadly weapons at their disposal, even doomsday tools if they are available. The function of armies has always been to overwhelm the opponent, and the manner of this overwhelming has rarely been of military concern. Part of the confusion stems from the belief that soldiers in war are like police fighting domestic crime. Police forces have a task of keeping potential offenders in line or of arresting those who will later be tried in court for possible punishment. Police are not supposed to kill the accused before a trial. Soldiers, on the other hand, shoot first and let others worry about questions of guilt later. No intention of ever conducting a trial exists for the soldier. The offenders and the police are citizens of the same country and subject to the same laws. Consequently, no one was surprised that police faced limits. Citizens are allowed a wide latitude of anarchic behavior before the police are called in. Police are not expected to curb every action off the norm. This is especially the case in matters of religion, economics, or politics. A democratic society has room for communists, socialists, anarchists, Protestants, Roman Catholics, atheists, and skin heads. Police are not supposed to wage ideological war, although during the McCarthy era and in the case of the supposed "moral majority" ideological repression was engaged in. Under more traditional American moments, however, such actions as attempted by the Ku Klux Klan, the John Birch Society, or the Moral Majority were generally seen as immoral, illegal, and unacceptable. In the international scene nations still operate at the level of crusade mentality. In spite of the warning of Victoria in the sixteenth century that wars over religion (ideology) should be absolutely forbidden, modern national groups wage wars with crusading zeal against economic theories, as well as political or religious differences. Wars are fought to make the world safe from capitalism, communism, theism, democracy, and fascism. Even our own national leaders have warned us that communist nations are "evil empires," with the implication that a violent crusade against them would be morally justified. Soldiers are praised for conducting inquisitions without murmur. This is not the case with police. The existence of this ideological McCarthyism in the international arena has led modern nations to hold the entire planet hostage to their aims. A current military writer spoke in praise of this unfortunate crusading zeal:

o   The communist enemy can be considered an international outlaw.

o   ...because of the nature of the communist enemy, our moral stance on the doctrine of the use of force need be only minimal.[12]

Armies are thus called upon to wage wars for reasons which our American politicians would normally blush to offer in sending police into action in our society.

The military establishment does not deserve sole blame for the general callousness with regard to what happens in wars against "saracens." Our leaders of state must share this responsibility along with businesses which make war products and sell them with free enterprise enthusiasm, and with the workers who profit from the entire business. Some national religious bodies have taken strong stands against nuclear weapons and even against some of the so-called conventional ones, but the average parishioner is no more sensitive to the humane issues of modern war than the average soldier in uniform. The Nuremberg judges were only too well aware of this in prosecuting those who actually operated the extermination camps, since, in a familiar economic tradition, they were only doing their job and making a living. The armaments business is immensely profitable. Drugs are probably the only other business that comes close to the armaments industry in the profits which can be made while offering no constructive contribution to society. Government "watchdog" committees exist to keep track of the drug traffic, but no one watches the firms which manufacture and promote nerve gas, napalm, chemical bombs, germ bombs, or nuclear bombs. Weapons which no police force would ever be permitted to buy or use become commonplace for soldiers. Thus, from the ordinary military perspective the Nuremberg Trials were no more than "victor's justice"; they set no restrictions on war making and were not viewed as having set any precedent. In our system of checks and balances, Congress and the White House might check each other, but no one adequately checks the Pentagon, the DOD, the CIA, or the arms industries. Instead of the constitutional provision for Congress to declare wars, such approvals are now made in secret without even Congress or the President knowing, by the State Department, the Department of Defense, and the Central Intelligence Agency. The military in the U.S. has assumed the political right to wage and declare wars as they see fit. Indeed, this military-industrial complex has replaced constitutional government in the United States in the matter of war.

VIETNAM: THE AMERICAN TRAGEDY

As General Telford Taylor pointed out in his book *Nuremberg and Vietnam: An American Tragedy*, the Vietnam war symbolized all of the difficulty of identifying laws of war, crimes of war, or crimes against humanity. The Vietnam war illustrated the dilemmas, including the gulf between what the army permitted and what Nuremberg had forbidden. It showed what moral crises can happen when a war of ideology is undertaken, and it showed that even a democratic country like the U.S. cannot afford to be led astray by moral crusaders. One thing which could be said about wars for property or aggrandizement was that they rarely had the breast-beating pharisaism of moral crusaders. Nations battled over land, and took the land as the prize for winning. War under the impetus of the search for natural resources like oil, rubber, or timber were motivated by economic greed and illustrated the capitalist virtues of a market competition. But the official justification for the Vietnam War was stripped of the obvious stake of the French and American rubber interests and it was presented to the American public as a holy war to save the world from communism. This element of crusading zeal led ultimately to the waging of the war by Americans with the utmost indifference to the combatant-non-combatant distinction, as if the Nuremberg Trials had never been held.

In the text of one of the reports by the Fulbright Committee on Foreign Relations with regard to the massive bombing of North Vietnam, the author, Robert Biles, observed,

> the objectives to be gained by bombing North Vietnam have varied during the course of the war, but they can be summarized as follows: 1) to reduce the infiltration of men and supplies to South Vietnam, 2) to make North Vietnam pay a high cost for supporting the war in the South, 3) to break the will of North Vietnam, 4) to effect negotiations for an end to the war, and 5) to raise U.S. and South Vietnamese morale.[13]

All five of these ends required using civilians as hostages, and surely this was what Nuremberg had confirmed was a crime against humanity. Senator Fulbright noted in his prefatory remarks that none of the five aims was ever fulfilled, and that in spite of this the massive and pointless bombing continued. The only results were great needless casualties among North Vietnamese civilians, the loss of many American lives, and the serious loss of moral standing of America in the world.

The distinguished historian of war, Quincy Wright, considered that seven questions needed to be answered before Vietnam could be put in legal or moral perspective.[14]

- o Was Vietnam a civil war? He concluded that it was and that the U.S. was then guilty of aggression in its invasion.

- o Did the proposed Vietnamese elections of 1956 depend on some prior conditions favorable to "free elections," or did the Geneva Accords intend an election with no preconditions? The latter was his conclusion.

- o Was the North an aggressor in its invasion of the South? He concluded that since North and South were one country the charge of aggression could not properly be made.

- o Did the Gulf of Tonkin Resolution of Congress of August 1, 1964 authorize the President to send American troops? Wright said that it did not.

- o Did the U.S. have any legal commitments to South Vietnam prior to February, 1965, to use armed forces in its defense? Wright noted that no American President ever recognized such a legal commitment.

- o Were the U.S. reprisals against North Vietnam in violation of international law? Wright concluded that they were, and even if they had not been, they were all out of proportion to the claimed offenses.

In 1976 Senator George McGovern made a report to the Committee on Foreign Relations of the Senate on Vietnam. By that time the Vietnam story was in the public domain, and it was timely for him to comment:

> We must have learned by now particularly after our experience with the People's Republic of China and with Cuba, that it is a self-defeating policy to wage economic and political warfare against countries simply because we consider that it was somehow unfair of their new rulers to prevail over those we preferred.[15]

The major elements of crimes of aggression and crimes against the peace were to be found in the American role in Vietnam. The U.S. had intervened in a civil war situation, created in part by the defeat of the French at Dienbienphu, and the U.S. had intervened on behalf of a wealthy and unrepresentative status quo. In response to Dean Rusk Senator McGovern remarked wryly,

> After all, Vietnam, is their country. We do not even have the right the French did. We have no historical right. We are obviously intruders from their point of view.[16]

By waging the Vietnam War America was committed to crimes against the peace, of a war of aggression. The guerrilla setting and the absence of established military fronts in this domestic people's war led to the breakdown of most of the prohibitions which had been laid down at The Hague and Geneva. Jean-Paul Sartre commented at the time of the Stockholm Tribunal that this, "people's war sounded the death-knell of conventional warfare exactly the same moment as the hydrogen bomb."[17] Richard Falk noted that not only did guerrilla war make conventional war rules inoperable, but the new strategies for waging guerrilla war made war crimes inevitable. Counterguerrilla strategy can proceed only,

> if it is based on an extraordinary ratio of military superiority, resulting in a degree of destruction and disruption disproportionate to the value of the political objectives.[18]

The Committee of Concerned Asian Scholars estimated that the kill ratio of civilians to soldiers was on the magnitude of ten to one. Every citizen of Vietnam was seen as a combatant with the result that a kind of "mass murder was accepted as legitimate."[19] It was revealing though macabre for Air Force Major Chester L. Brown to say after the bombing of Ben Tre, "it became necessary to destroy the town in order to save it."[20] Few industrial targets and no clear military targets existed. Neither The Hague nor Geneva prohibitions could survive this kind of wholesale and indiscriminate slaughter. The casualty reports from Vietnam were filled predominantly with civilians, and no military way of avoiding this seemed available. After the U.S. had bombed Quang Ngai, May 31, 1965, an estimated 500 Vietnamese were killed. The official American report was that they were soldiers of the Vietcong. Yet, a report from a group of medical doctors stationed there at the time affirmed,

Three out of four patients seeking treatment in a Vietnamese hospital afterward for burns from napalm and jellied gasoline, were village women.[21]

Some American defenders tried to dismiss American responsibility for these kinds of killings on the grounds that it was the fault of the enemy for waging guerrilla war.[22] But the fact remained that from the perspective of Nuremberg this was a policy of planned crimes against humanity. General Telford Taylor, who had played so important a role at those Trials, was dismayed by what the Americans had done in Vietnam and he considered the entire affair a great tragedy.[23]

A military commission under the leadership of General Peers found evidence that at every level within the military steps had been taken to suppress the information as to what had happened, especially at My Lai and Son My. The Commission noted,

> Six officers who occupied key positions at the time of the incident exercised their right to remain silent before this Inquiry, others gave false or misleading testimony or withheld information, and key documents relating to the incident have not been found in the U.S. files. [24]

Thirty officers and one enlisted man were charged with these offenses: 1 Major General, 1 Brigadier General, 4 Colonels, 2 Lieutenant Colonels, 3 Majors, 8 Captains, 4 First Lieutenants, 6 Second Lieutenants, 1 Sergeant, and 1 Private. Only three were brought to trial: Private Schwartz, Sergeant Hutto, and Lieutenant Calley. The rest were acquitted without further prosecution other than being named by the Peers Commission of inquiry. None of the three was tried under the Nuremberg Charter. Instead, each was tried under *The Uniform Code of Military Justice*.[25] The cases revolved around the question of superior orders and of whether the actions performed were of the type the normal soldier would have known were illegal. Sergeant Hutto was cleared of all charges. In the trial of Private Michael Schwartz, decided October 29, 1971, Senior Judge Morgan ruled that while Private Schwartz was properly charged with the premeditated murder of sixteen Vietnamese civilians in violation of the UCMJ, Article 118, the case was ruled to be non-capital.[26] While the initial sentence was life imprisonment at hard labor, forfeiture of all pay allowances, and dishonorable discharge, the final disposition reduced the sentence to one year at hard labor, forfeiture of pay, and dishonorable discharge.

The publicity was greatest in the Calley case. The court martial found him guilty, March 29, 1971, of murdering 102 unarmed Vietnamese civilians, and gave him a life term in prison. There was a public outcry in defense of Calley, and President Nixon ordered his release from prison pending review. He was restricted to quarters during this period. President Nixon was criticized by both the legal and military authorities for undermining the court martial system. In August, 1971 his sentence was reduced to 20 years, the same sentence given to Albert Speer at Nuremberg. The 20 year sentence was further reduced to 10 years with eligibility for parole. On September 25, 1974 the Calley conviction was overturned by the U.S. District Court in Columbus, Georgia and his release was ordered. In 1975 the conviction was reinstated but he was not returned to prison since he had only ten days left before his parole. He had already begun a lecture circuit in the spring of 1975 speaking at Murray State University for a fee of $2,000 about his experiences.

The only other serious efforts to evaluate and judge the role of the United States in Vietnam were unofficial. The D.R.V.N. (Democratic Republic of North Vietnam) conducted a Commission for the Investigation of U.S. Imperialist War Crimes in Vietnam. The Commission, being North Vietnamese, was obviously in no position to get those charged to appear before its court. There was also a Tokyo Tribunal organized by the Japanese philosopher, Yoshishige Kosai, held in August, 1967. The most famous of these unofficial efforts were those conducted at Stockholm, Sweden and Rothskilde, Denmark. These had been initiated by the philosophers, Jean-Paul Sartre and Bertrand Russell. Between May 2 and 10, 1967 this International War Crimes Tribunal met at Stockholm. The Tribunal considered two questions: 1) Did the U.S., Australia, New Zealand, and South Korea commit acts of international aggression according to international law? and 2) Had there been a bombardment of targets of a purely civilian nature, such as schools, hospitals, dams, etc., and on what scale did these bombings occur? In support of the contention that the four nations had participated in prohibited acts of war the Tribunal followed the precedent of Nuremberg citing the following kinds of evidence:

o The Paris Pact had outlawed war.

o Article 2 of the U.N. Charter reaffirmed the Paris Pact.

o Article 6 of the Nuremberg Charter had identified aggressive war as in violation of treaties.

o The United Nations Resolution of December, 1960, had obligated members not to wage aggressive war.

o The Geneva Accords had forbidden any invasion of Vietnam by American troops.[27]

Utilizing these documents as the bases for crimes against the peace, and citing evidence of the actions of the United States to the contrary, the Stockholm Tribunal ruled that the U.S. had been guilty of aggression in Vietnam and that it had thereby committed crimes against the peace. The vote was unanimous for the verdict of guilt. With respect to the charge that the United States had deliberately waged war against civilian populations, the Tribunal appealed to The Hague Convention of October 18, 1907, which had established, sufficiently for use at Nuremberg, that belligerents did not have unlimited choice of means to injure the enemy. Article 23 of that Convention prohibited weapons that caused unnecessary suffering; Article 25 forbade the attack on undefended towns; Article 27 forbade the bombardment of hospitals, churches, schools, museums, and historical monuments. The Tribunal also cited Article 6 of the Statutes of the Nuremberg Tribunal which had classified the bombing of civilian targets as a crime, and Article 18 of the Geneva Convention which had made the same prohibition. The Stockholm Tribunal even cited the U.S. Army manual, *The Law of Land Warfare* in its support. Based on the testimony at the Trials the Tribunal, again by unanimous decision, found all four nations guilty as charged.

From November 30 through December 1, 1967 the Tribunal met in Rothskilde. At these second sessions the Tribunal made the following charges.

o Japan, Thailand, and the Philippines were accomplices in the acts of aggression committed by the United States.

o Weapons which were forbidden by the laws of war were used.

o Prisoners of war were maltreated.

o The war was extended to Laos.

o The U.S. was probably guilty of the charge of genocide, at least as far as killing communists was concerned.

In its verdict, the Rothskilde Tribunal concluded that the governments of Thailand and the Philippines were guilty by a unanimous decision. The government of Japan was ruled guilty of complicity by a vote of 8 to 3. The U.S. was ruled guilty by a unanimous decision of crimes against the people of Laos, of the use of forbidden weapons, of the maltreatment of prisoners of war, and of genocide.[28]

At the time of the trials testimony was received with respect to the use of fragmentation bombs against the Vietnamese. Jean-Pierre Vigier, M.D., Director of Research at the National Center for Scientific Research, and former Officer-in-Charge of Armaments Inspection for the French Army under General De Lattre de Tassigny, emphasized the essentially indiscriminate nature of these anti-personnel weapons. They could not, in any sense, be aimed, and they exploded in a 360 degree radius. This fact, combined with the absence of any genuine military targets, meant that civilians would have no protection. He reported,

> The primary objective of the bombing is the people them-
> selves. That's, I believe, why fragmentation bombs have been
> used in such high proportion: 50% of all bombs falling on
> North Vietnam are fragmentation bombs. This is not an
> accident: this is the logical application of U.S. theory of
> military weapons against an under-developed country.[29]

The Tribunal also received a Combined Report on Anti-Personnel Bombs by Members of the Japanese Scientific Committee which had paid special attention to the "ball bombs" (fragmentation or cluster bombs). The Report noted that the bombs did no harm to military hardware, they were designed to kill or maim as many as possible, and they inflicted injuries extremely hard to treat. The Report compared them to dum dum bullets in their inhumaneness, causing relatively little damage on entry but immense damage inside the body.[30] The Pentagon claimed on May 5, 1967 that it was not using these Cannister Bombs against civilian targets, but the evidence was to the contrary. We know that these weapons were available because they were listed as part of the available arsenal in the Department of the Army *Chemical Reference Handbook. FM 38.*[31] Furthermore, the medical doctors had treated civilians for wounds from these weapons. *Aviation Week* in February, 1967 affirmed that the bombs were normally dropped from planes at an altitude of three miles, so that the claim that civilians were being carefully avoided was absurd. What the Vietnam war had shown was that normal or conventional war practices were indistinguishable from crimes against humanity in the clear Nuremberg sense of the terms. Yet, most officers seemed unaware of this.

The Citizens Commission of Inquiry under the Dellums Committee Hearings interviewed Vietnam veterans to see whether the My Lai-like practices were standard or exceptional, and to determine, if possible, whether officers had received training at their respective war colleges on where they were expected to draw the humanitarian limits. The results were dismaying. Captain Fred Laughlin, U.S. Army, Class of 1965 at West Point, thought that the expression "war crime" made no sense since war required the repudiation of all laws.[32] Major Gorson Livingston, U.S. Army, Class of 1960 at West Point, said that the American practice of torturing Vietnamese prisoners was finally stopped because it was unproductive rather than because of any sense of humanitarian outrage.[33] Captain Robert B. Johnson, U.S. Army, Class of 1965 at West Point, said, "I did not know what the law of land warfare was until I returned from Vietnam in 1969."[34] Lance Corporal Kenneth Campbell said,

> never during the course of my enlisted service... nor as an officer did I receive any instruction regarding the Hague or Geneva Conventions, the Nuremberg Principles, or the treatment of POWs.[35]

To see if these were isolated instances or exceptional cases, a survey was made of the U.S. war colleges, prompted by the apparent confusion among American soldiers as to the requirements of the laws of war.[36] The question was: are the laws of war taught to soldiers in the official war colleges? At the Naval War College in 1971 a series of talks on international law was given chiefly by visitors. In the winter term an elective seminar was offered on some topic of international law. It met thirteen times. In the spring a further elective seminar was offered. The National War College had no required course in international law. The Air War College had one one-hour lecture a year. The Army War College had twelve lectures by a resident professor. The Air Force Academy at Colorado Springs in 1979 had a serious course on "War and Morality" in which students were exposed to articles by non-military writers, a divergence from the general lack of such topics in other military colleges.

Guilt or uneasiness concerning the Vietnam war was not generally voiced. Captain William H. Miller remarked that he felt guilty about the many My-Lai type operations he had participated in, and stated that such operations would continue as long as the government in the U.S. continued on its course of action abroad.[37] Captain Greg Howard, U.S. Army Class of 1964 West Point had worked under General Ewell whose division had an unsurpassed record of "body count," and he referred to the manner of killing the Vietnamese as "killing fish in a barrel."[38] He found it ironic that General Ewell was the American military representative at the Paris Peace Talks. Martin Gershen, on the contrary, denied that anything criminal had occurred at My Lai and that the events were simply the result of mechanical or human error.[39] Lieutenant Calley was surprised that he was tried.

> I thought, could it be that I did something wrong?...I had killed, but I knew so did a million others. I sat there and I couldn't find the key. I pictured the people of My Lai: the bodies, and they didn't bother me....Killing those men at My Lai didn't haunt me.[40]

If any lesson comes from My Lai it is that the entire subject of laws of war was so unclear in the minds of soldiers and politicians alike that Nuremberg must have seemed like a mistake. If Nuremberg had set any precedent at all for Americans, then it should have led to official war crimes trials comparable to the ones held at Stockholm and Rothskilde.

THE PRODUCT OF DERANGED MINDS?

This question arose at the time of the Nuremberg Trials and psychiatrists came up with diametrically opposed conclusions. At one extreme the thesis was proferred that the Nazi atrocities had been committed by normal persons under the harassing conditions of war. At the other extreme, the thesis was that the Nazis were mentally unbalanced sadists.

The first position, that the gas chamber operators and death camp torturers were simply ordinary husbands and wives, who during the rest of their lives behaved like conventionally polite and loving citizens, had some supporting evidence. Hannah Arendt covered the Eichmann Trial in Jerusalem in 1961 for *The New Yorker* magazine. She spoke of the "banality of evil," noting that with regard to Eichmann,

> half a dozen psychiatrists certified him as 'normal' more normal at any rate, than I am after having examined him, one of them... had found his whole attitude toward his wife and children, mother and father... was not only "normal," but most desirable. [41]

The minister who visited him said that he was a man with very "positive" ideas. But people did not want to believe that an average person could be so incapable of knowing right from wrong. Arendt concluded, "The trouble with Eichmann was precisely that so many were like him, and that many were neither perverted or sadistic."[42]

Albert Speer, one of the Germans found guilty by the Nuremberg Court, observed that he was the only Nazi who admitted guilt and responsibility.[43] Did the rest of the Germans feel no guilt because they were abnormal or was it simply that in times of war normal persons can be trained to do abnormal deeds? This normality thesis was the subject of a study made by Stanley Milgram at Yale. Milgram wanted to discover the extent to which normal persons would obey orders which conflicted with their conscience. Volunteers were hired as "teachers" and paid actors were hired as "patients." The volunteers were told that the aim of the study was to determine how to improve learning and memory. They were seated at a "shock generator" with dials simulated to increase voltage from 15 to 450 volts. The teacher was to administer shock in increasing doses when the "learner" made mistakes. The "learners" simulated pain. Not a single "teacher" refused to raise the voltage up to 300 volts, and 65 percent increased the voltage up to the maximum at which time the "patients" appeared to become unconscious. Milgram concluded that when individuals operate in an "organizational mode" they do not assess the morality of the orders they receive.[44] The normality thesis received further support from a study of the twenty-two Nazis charged at Nuremberg. D.M. Kelley concluded that while many of them were not what one would call normal, they were all "essentially sane... although in some instances somewhat deviated from normal."[45]

With respect to the second thesis, support existed for the theory that the Nazis were "deviants." Gustave M. Gilbert administered the Rorschach tests to the accused at Nuremberg and concluded that based on these tests the men were clearly deviants. While holding to the deviant hypothesis Gilbert, stated that the

> Nazi movement was not solely the product of the distinctive pathological characteristics of men.... Not every psychopath, after all, becomes a Nazi, and not every Nazi was a psycho-path. [46]

But we need to remember that the war crimes trials were not conducted on any premise that the accused were insane. They were not prosecuted on the assumption that they were psychologically sick. They were prosecuted for being normal persons who should have refused to be a party to the exterminations. They were not mental patients but over-zealous patriots. A similar position was supplied by Peter Karsten who concluded that many of the offenders at My Lai had brought crude and brutal values into the army with them. Some were persons whose "normal" social attitude regarded darker-skinned persons as less than human. In addition, the war environment always tends to make otherwise decent persons commit what in peace time they would recognize as atrocities. He concluded that some of the commanding officers in Vietnam were not the type who should have been given command. The solution he suggested was to weed out sadists, give more training on laws of war, have better weapons review, and help soldiers cope with the problem of obedience to illegal orders.[47] But this fails to take account of the history of warfare. We have limited commitment to laws of war precisely because of the military unwillingness to accept any restrictions based on moral considerations. An abysmal review of weapons is the established military intention. No matter what the psychic health of the soldier, he must either become accustomed to atrocities or become ill as a result of what he is commanded to do. It is unrealistic to imagine that an army of mentally fit soldiers could still avoid committing some of the crimes of war. Our indiscriminate weapons require this result. What is finally at issue is whether military necessity will ever give in to moral reservations.

IS THERE ANY RESOLUTION?

Can we ever solve the dilemma between the demands of sovereign nations to wage wars in their national interest and the moral concern that wars not cause more damage than the imaginable gain? Can we ever be serious again about the prohibitions of The Hague and Geneva conventions that stirred the creation of the Nuremberg Charter? If all prohibitions advocated by The Hague, Geneva, or United Nations resolutions must first have the prior approval of the military establishment before they can become rules of war, will rules of war ever exist? Must we continue to deplore the "atrocities" committed by our enemies while remaining blind to the atrocities implicit in how we all wage modern war? Must every succeeding war crimes trial be an exercise in Philistine breast-beating? While it would be naive to imagine that any simple or palatable solution could be found, it would be needlessly pessimistic to conclude that war must remain forever outside of the normal moral checks and balances which the human race has developed for curbing domestic atrocities. The cures may transcend present willingness to accept, but the major causes surrounding the moral malaise are not mysteries.

Part of the solution lies in correcting the present partnership of the military-industrial-political complex. This unfortunate collusion of disparate processes has played a major role in determining foreign policy, committing our nation to increasing escalation of weapons, making the "weapons reviews," and supplying the spokespersons at "peace" and "disarmament" talks. The first two parties, military and industrial, have usurped the major role and have conducted foreign affairs in secret from Congress, the American public, the press, and even the White House. Our founding fathers never intended this kind of military-industrial guidance, nor did they expect a secret group of military planners, such as exists in the Pentagon, the Department of Defense, and the Central Intelligence Agency. Both Germany and Japan suffered from this same unholy alliance. Much as we claim to deplore the military takeover in Third World countries, we must now admit that both the U.S.S.R. and the United States have become victims of a massive military-industrial coup. The normal democratic processes have been subverted, and we, like Japan and Germany, have been guided by disciples of Clausewitz rather than of Jefferson. As long as this remains the case and this power group is permitted to promote its aims, pass on the legitimacy of its strategies, influence foreign affairs, plot and carry out revolutions abroad in the name of the United States, and at the same time conceal all this from Congress and the public in the name of "national defense," it will be idle to complain about the crimes of war. Neither the American nor the Soviet military-industrial complexes will be any more likely than the Japanese or German complexes were to police their own operations or to be morally selective in choosing either the ends or means for which patriotic battle is warranted.

This same complex is an ideological and missionary one with the same blind zeal which characterized the medieval crusaders. Nazis were willing to play the role of inquisitors because of their doctrine of Aryan supremacy. Current American zealots exhibit the same willingness because of their doctrine of communist evil and capitalist virtue. Nations would probably be less dangerous, and less likely to make war on the innocent, were they to wage wars solely out of lust for empire or greed for the natural resources of their neighbors. The crusade against communism runs the same risks as the crusade against the heathen did, because both crusades demean their opponents as immoral or evil monsters. This belief, in turn, justifies every atrocity. Roman Catholic leaders used to believe that unless the world was converted to their sentiments no hope would exist for mankind. We now know that this is an absurd idea. Indeed, when the United Nations was first formed, many with an inquisitor mentality doubted that nations of disparate ideologies would ever be able to talk with each other. How could monarchists, democrats, socialists, communists, capitalists, dictators, and feudal barons find any common bases for agreement? But if the United Nations has demonstrated anything well it is that ideological differences do not preclude agreements on some matters like world health, a world bank, the condemnation of genocide, or the unacceptable nature of weapons of "mass destruction." Moral sensitivity is not restricted to the "enlightened" West. The basic disagreements among nation states are not ideological. They are based on economic and political power struggles. It took great courage and diligence before the inquisition of McCarthyism was rooted out, and something comparable is required in the international scene. Waging wars is a risky enough business without the issues being inflamed by ideological fervor.

It has been all too easy to forget that it was the German military-industrial-political complex which was prosecuted at Nuremberg. This was the group which conspired, plotted, and waged the aggressive and inhumane policies for which they were found guilty. It was the religious bigotry of Nazism which lay at the root of the problem, coupled with simple Clausewitzian thinking. This missionary fervor which leads to the inquisitorial mentality may flower in both fascist and democratic climates. The Nazis proposed the "final solution" to rid themselves of the perceived threat of the non-Aryans. Americans have as easily proposed nuclear annihilation to rid themselves of the perceived threat of communism. What Aryan supremacy as a dogma did for Germany, anti-communism as a dogma can do for the United States. How else can we explain the willingness of the Department of Defense and the Central Intelligence Agency to conduct medical experiments on American citizens and wage terrorist forays into other countries? How else can we explain the passive acceptance of basically anti-civilian weapons like napalm, fragmentation bombs, chemical/biological warfare, and nuclear bombs if not because our national leaders, and the citizens themselves, have willingly committed us to a holy war against our economic enemies? Many of the crimes of war are the result of this passionate, if misguided, patriotism.

The military manuals have come in for sufficient criticism in these pages. Under the limitations with which armies are asked to operate, and given the advice, or lack thereof, of national political bodies, these manuals are remarkable documents. The language of concern appears in them. The rules which could serve to limit the worst havoc of war are, for the most part, named therein. What makes the problem of balancing moral concern with the necessities of being an army at all, are the three military dogmas: military necessity, the right of reprisal, and the obligation of soldiers to obey superior orders without question. We can understand why some orders need to be obeyed. No alternative to this would permit a functioning army. What we need, however, is some way to evaluate the orders on the part of those at the top who initiate them. Police manuals are not asked to solve this thorny question, and we cannot expect army manuals to do so. The quality of war orders is a moral matter, even if the carrying out of the orders is a military one. If the doctrine of military necessity will not be abandoned, then the calculations of what is militarily necessary must be made elsewhere than by the military itself. Part of the difficulty in a democracy is to identify which groups should be entrusted to make these basic moral decisions. How far should Americans be willing to go to achieve their perceived national ends? How far should the peoples of any nation be willing to go? Something comparable to the giving up of states' rights on the domestic scene is needed internationally. The experience in the United Nations Organization has illustrated how difficult it has been for nations to relinquish sovereignty. Crusaders do not give in to saracens, nor do they possess the kind of moral plurality which would prompt them to set aside the first stone.

The nuclear confrontation, with the attendant attempts for superiority, leads to a race which many experts admit can never be won. Many experts agree that if the U.S. were to scrap all its nuclear armaments save those on nuclear submarines, national security would remain unaffected.[48] We could still return this planet to the stone age. Yet we manufacture new nuclear weapons weekly even though the additional ones offer no further military protection.

The Nuremberg judges believed laws of war could be derived from proclamations from The Hague and Geneva. United Nations Resolutions, which are more international than The Hague or Geneva resolutions ever were, must not be dismissed as many ardent nationalists propose. At the U.N. nations stand up and are counted. Nations cast a ballot, and the world can see where they stand. Discussions are open and public, unlike so-called peace conferences held at Geneva. The votes in the U.N. showed us where nations stood on "weapons of mass destruction," genocide, a ban on nuclear testing, chemical/biological warfare, and the nuclear arms race. In the U.N. nations have to take a stand and bear the brunt of whatever moral indignation the other nations might express. If leaders of the world want to know where peoples stand on the moral issues of war, as yet no better place exists than in the arena of the United Nations. America cannot hold its head above a vote of 83 to 3 against genocide, when we are one of the three nations opposed to the resolution. Any claim to being a moral leader is disqualified by this kind of vote. Ideally, Congress and the White House bear the heaviest blame. Our leaders need to go to New York before they flee to Geneva in search of moral support for rules of war.

It was understood by jurists by the end of the eighteenth century that the ends of sovereign nationalism were inconsistent with the hope for laws of war. The result has been that just war concerns have vanished save as an academic topic. The time has come to see that modern weapons and strategies are inconsistent with any plausible meaning to the existence of laws of war. Moderation has become a meaningless term. The combatant-non-combatant distinction has vanished. We gave up the belief in laws of war once we lost our sense of proportionality in weapons. The sophistry of pretending otherwise was no better illustrated than in the expression "limited nuclear war."

We gave up this sense of proportionality long before the advent of atomic weapons. If Pope Innocent III was sufficiently outraged at careless slaughter to recommend banning the crossbow, it took Pope John XXIII the atomic bomb before he expressed comparable concern. If even papal leaders can acclimatize themselves to napalm, flame throwers, fragmentation bombs, and chemical/biological weapons perhaps little should be expected of their laity. We are expected to be patriots before we are moral persons, with the consequence that laws of war will be defeated from the start. It isn't that there are no believers in laws of war, or that no international laws exist, but that the demands of sovereign nationalism require leaders to ignore the laws. National leaders show support for such laws only when it is in their national interest to do so. This was why even at the sober meetings at The Hague provision was made for nations to be excused from compliance with the conventions when it was against their national interest to do so.

It isn't that military manuals show no regard for the fate of both soldiers and civilians in time of war. Noble sentiments can be found in *The Law of Land Warfare*. But this is an area where military-political expertise and training are no asset. We need moral assessments of ends and means. Every civilization has already codified its domestic moral limits and created some kind of calculus for what would be proportional. Domestically no American leader would be praised for using chemical/biological weapons, let alone napalm, fragmentation bombs, or aerial bombardment in New York city or Atlanta to solve the problems of drugs or discrimination however pressing they might be. No American leader could recommend that ghettos be bombed to "save them" as was done in Vietnam. We suffer many things at home in order not to lose our self-respect and respect for others. But little of this laboriously developed moral sensitivity has been translated into foreign affairs. Nations behave like callous vigilantes toward each other. Leaders in the most respected positions speak like moral Frankensteins. They find the horrors of war "thinkable" under the most shallow of *tu quoque* arguments. What would be branded as child sacrifice at home is standard military practice with regard to our neighbor's children.

We know what should be done and what ought not to be done. Non-combatants should be spared, unfortified cities ought not to be bombed, unnecessary suffering should be avoided, the wounded and imprisoned should be cared for, and every alternative short of war should be thoroughly exhausted first. But as long as sovereign nations retain the inalienable inhuman right to defend their ends, and to be the sole judges of those ends, no manual will ever be written that would really guide soldiers to avoid crimes against humanity and crimes of war. The twin doctrines of military necessity and national sovereignty will continue to erase all potential laws of war.

It has been all too easy to forget that the laws of war with which contemporary armies are expected to comply were written for a time when the weapons of war were relatively simple. The cavalry of the Russian army in World War I went faster and farther than the best Russian tanks. Cannon projectiles might contain as much as fifty pounds of high explosive, but current bombs are a billion times more powerful. We have airplanes with unthought of speed and intercontinental missiles which allow no time for defense. Incendiaries, gas, and chemicals which had been historically banned are all standard in military arsenals. Although the manuals still speak of chivalry as if it were an ameliorating force, the language of knighthood no longer has any meaning. Indeed, if medieval knights had done battle with flame throwers, poison gas, fragmentation bombs or the M1 rifle, the term chivalry would never have arisen. The indiscriminateness of "conventional" weapons used by the armies of the world, quite apart from nuclear weapons, now requires us to conclude that what we do on the battlefield is not war at all. If rules could reasonably be written for nineteenth century war, these same rules make no moral sense today. Rules of war to calculate the proportionality of nineteenth century weapons have no meaning in the twentieth century. If war ever was the "extension of politics" what we now practice surely is not. Some world organization, however repugnant to sovereign nationalists, is a wiser course to pursue than to pretend that we are still defending national security by waging war when we are actually committing international suicide while at the same time justifying genocide.

NOTES

1. *The Law of Land Warfare*, paragraph 3a.

2. Tertullian, *On Idolatry*, Ch. XIX.

3. Desiderius Erasmus, *The Complaint of Peace* (New York: Scholar's Facsimile and Reprints, 1946), pp. 17-23.

4. George Fox, *Journal*, pp. 356-357 and 400 (London: W. Richardson and S. Clark, 1765).

5. Leo Tolstoy, "Nobel's Bequest," in *Essays, Letters and Miscellanies* (London: Oxford University Press, 1936), Vol. II, P. 1.

6. Emil Brunner, *The Divine Imperative* (Philadelphia: Westminster Press, 1947), p. 469.

7. John C. Bennett, *Christians and the State* (New York: Charles Scribner's Sons, 1958), p. 179.

8. Reinhold Niebuhr, *Christianity and Power Politics* (New York: Charles Scribner's Sons, 1940), p. 4.

9. Emmerich Vattel, *The Law of Nations* (Washington: Carnegie Foundation, 1916), Ch. VIII, paragraph 138.

10. Cf. J.M. Spaight, *War Rights on Land* (New York: Macmillan, 1911), p. 78.

11. S.L.A. Marshall, *Men Against Fire* (Gloucester, Mass.: Peter Smith, 1964).

12. Captain Paul R. Schratz, U.S. Navy (Ret.) "War, Morality and the Military Profession," *Military Law Review* (September, 1983), p. 48.

13. "Bombing as a Policy Tool in Vietnam Effectiveness." A Staff Study Based on the Pentagon Papers. Prepared for the U.S. Senate Committee on Foreign Relations. Study 5 (October 12, 1972), p. 1.

14. Quincy Wright, "Legal Aspects of the Vietnam Situation," *The American Journal of International Law*, Vol. 60 (October, 1966).

15. *Vietnam 1976.* A Report by Senator George McGovern (March, 1976). U.S. Government Printing Office, 94th Congress, 2nd Session, p. 1.

16. William J. Fulbright, *The Vietnam Hearings* (New York: Random House, 1966), p. 283.

17. Jean-Paul Sartre, "On Genocide." Cited in Paul T. Menzel (ed.), *Moral Argument and the War in Vietnam* (Nashville: Aurora Press, 1971), p. 62.

18. Richard A. Falk, *The Status of Law in International Society* (Princeton: Princeton University Press, 1970), pp. 584-585.

19. Richard A. Falk, Gabriel Kolko, and Robert Jay Lifton (eds.), *Crimes of War* (New York: Random House, 1971), pp. 459-460.

20. The Committee of Concerned Asian Scholars, *The Indochina Story* (New York: Random House, 1970), pp. 128-129.

21. Jack Langguth, "Saigon, South Vietnam," *New York Times* (June 1, 1965).

22. David Little, "Is the War in Vietnam Just?" in Paul T. Menzel (ed.), *Moral Argument and the War In Vietnam* (Nashville: Aurora Press, 1971), p. 12.

23. Richard A. Falk, *The Vietnam War* (Princeton: Princeton University Press, 1976), p. 271.

24. Joseph Goldstein, Burke Marshall, and Jack Schwartz, *The My Lai Massacre and Its Cover-Up* (New York: Free Press, 1976), p. 52.

25. *Court Martial Reports.* Holdings and Decisions of the Courts of Military Review and the United States Court of Military Appeals, Vol. 46 (1971-1973), p. 1138.

26. *Ibid*, Vol. 45 (1971-1972), p. 854.

27. John Duffett (ed.), *Against the Crime of Silence: Proceedings of the International War Crimes Tribunal* (New York: Free Press, 1976), p. 302-305.

28. *Ibid.*, p. 309.

29. Jean-Pierre Vigier, M.D., "Technical Aspects of Fragmentation Bombs," Cited in Duffett, *ibid.*, p. 258.

30. *Ibid.*

31. *Ibid.*, p. 42.

32. *The Citizen's Commission of Inquiry: The Dellums Committee Hearings on War Crimes in Vietnam* (New York: Random House, 1972), pp. 10-12.

33. *Ibid.*, p. 33.

34. *Ibid.*, pp. 40-41.

35. *Ibid.*

36. L.F.E. Goldie, "International Law at the War Colleges," *The American Journal of International Law* Vol. 66. (January, 1972).

37. Cited in Falk, Kolko, and Lifton, (eds.), *Crimes of War.* pp. 395-396.

38. *The Citizen's Commission of Inquiry.* p. 42.

39. Martin Gershen, *Destroy or Die* (New Rochelle, N.Y.: Arlington House, 1971), pp. 301-302.

40. John Sack, *Lieutenant Calley: His Own Story* (New York: Viking, 1970), pp. 8, 104.

41. Hannah Arendt, *Eichmann In Jerusalem* (New York: Viking, 1964), p. 26.

42. *Ibid.*, p. 36.

43. Albert Speer, *Inside the Third Reich* (New York: Macmillan, 1976), p. 614.

44. Cited in Arendt, *Eichmann.* pp. 129-130.

45. D.M. Kelley, "Preliminary Studies of the Rorschach Records of Nazi War Criminals," *Rorschach Research Exchange* (1946), pp. 46-47.

46. The American Veterans Against the War, *The Winter Soldier Investigation* (Boston: Beacon Press, 1972), p. 282.

47. Peter Karsten, *Law, Soldiers and Combat* (Westport, Conn.: Greenwood, 1978).

48. Cf. Paul H. Ehrlich, "Disarmament: The Lesser Risk," *The Bulletin of the Atomic Scientists* (August-September, 1982); Jerome B. Wiesner, "Is a Moratorium Safe?" *The Bulletin of Atomic Scientists* (August-September, 1982); Victor F. Weisskopf, "Nuclear War: Four Pressure Points," *The Bulletin of the Atomic Scientists* (January, 1982); Carl Sagan, "The Nuclear Winter," *Parade* (October 30, 1980); Gordon Adams, "What Do Weapons Secure?" *The Bulletin of the Atomic Scientists* (April, 1982); Christopher Paine, "The Elusive 'Margin of Safety,'" *The Bulletin of the Atomic Scientists* (May, 1982); Herbert York, "Vertical Proliferation," *The Bulletin of the Atomic Scientists* (December, 1982).

Appendix A
JUDGMENTS AT NUREMBERG

The accused were charged on four counts: 1) waging wars of aggression, 2) crimes against the peace, 3) war crimes, and 4) crimes against humanity. The judgments ranged from hanging to 'not guilty.' Two escaped final sentencing by suicide. One was not tried because of age, and two were found 'not guilty'.

Name	The Charges	The Sentence
Goering	1,2,3,4	hanging
Ribbentrop	1,2,3,4	hanging
Keitel	1,2,3,4	hanging
Rosenberg	1,2,3,4	hanging
Jodl	1,2,3,4	hanging
Seyss-Inquart	2,3,4	hanging
Kaltenbrunner	3,4	hanging
Frank	3,4	hanging
Sauckel	3,4	hanging
Bormann	3,4	hanging
Streicher	4	hanging
Funk	2,3,4	life
Raeder	1,2,3	life
Hess	1,2	life
Speer	3,4	20 years
Von Shiroch	4	20 years
Von Neurath	1,2,3,4	15 years
Doenitz	2,3	10 years
Fritzsche	2,3	pardoned
Von Papen		not guilty
Schacht		not guilty
Krupp		not tried
Ley		suicide
Conti		suicide

In Volume XXII of the forty-two volume set, *Trial of the Major War Criminals*. (Nuremberg, 1949), pp. 524-589, it was reported that on the 218th day of the Trials summation and sentence judgments were given. The decisions were also summarized in Robert H. Jackson, *Report to the International Conference on Military Trials*. (New York: AMS Press, 1971), pp. 422f.

Appendix B
TRIALS UNDER
CONTROL COUNCIL LAW NO.10

These were trials where the crimes had been committed in a specific locale. The major Allied powers divided tha areas among themselves and conducted only those trials in their respective areas. The following were conducted by the United States.

Each of these trials was identified by a class name, and in all but one case there were more than one accused.

Case Name	Indicted	Tried	Death	Life	Prison	Not Guilty
Einsatzgruppen	24	22	14	2	6	
Medical	23	23	7	5	4	7
Pohl	18	18	3	3	9	3
Justice	16	14		4	6	4
Hostage	12	10		2	6	2
High Command	14	13		2	9	2
Rusha	14	14		1	12	1
Ministries	21	21			19	2
Farben	24	23			13	10
Krupp	12	12			11	1
Flick	6	6			3	3
Milch	1	1		1		

Four committed suicide before their trials ended, and four were released from trial due to incompetence to stand trial.

These Trials were documented in *Trials of War Criminals Before the Nuerenberg Military Tribunals Under Control Council Law No. 10.* U.S. (Washington: U.S.Government Printing Office, 1949). The summation of these results was reported in Telford Taylor, *Final Report to Secretary of the Army on the Nuernberg War Crimes Trials Under Control Council Law No. 10.* (Washington: U.S. Government Printing Office, 1949)

Appendix C
JUDGMENTS AT TOKYO

Name	Number of Charges for Crimes Against the Peace	Atrocities	War Crimes	Sentence
Itigaki	8	no	yes	hanging
Dohihara	7	yes	no	hanging
Kimura	7	no	no	hanging
Tojo	6	yes	no	hanging
Muto	5	yes	yes	hanging
Hirata	2	no	yes	hanging
Matsui	0	no	yes	hanging
Koiso	5	no	yes	life
Sato	5	no	no	life
Shimada	5	no	no	life
Suzuki	5	no	no	life
Umezu	5	no	no	life
Oka	5	no	no	life
Kido	5	no	no	life
Kaya	5	no	no	life
Hoshino	5	no	no	life
Hashimoto	2	no	no	life
Araki	2	no	no	life
Minami	2	no	no	life
Oshima	1	no	no	life
Togo	5	no	no	20 yrs.
Shigemitsu	5	no	yes	7 yrs.

A complete listing of the charges and the judgments may be found in Solis Horowitz, "The Tokyo Trial," *International Conciliation* (Carnegie Endowment, Washington, D.C., November, 1950), No. 465, p. 584.

BIBLIOGRAPHY

Appleman, John Alan, *Military Tribunals and International Crimes* (Westport, Conn.: Greenwood Press, 1971).

Arendt, Hannah, *Eichmann In Jerusalem* (New York: Viking Press, 1963). New York, 1963.

_____, *The Origins of Totalitarianism* (New York: Harcourt, Brace and World, 1966).

Armed Forces Special Weapons Project, *Radiological Defense*, Volume II, *The Principles of Military Defense Against Atomic Weapons* (Washington: U.S. Government Printing Office, November, 1951).

Army Field Manual No. 21-13, *The Soldier's Guide* (Washington: U.S. Government Printing Office, August 22, 1961).

Army Field Manual No. 11-3, *Employment of Chemical and Biological Agents* (Washington: U.S. Government Printing Office, March 31, 1966).

Army Field Manual No. 3-8, *Chemical Reference Book* (Washington: U.S. Government Printing Office, January 6, 1967).

Army Field Manual, *Rules of Land Warfare* (Washington: U.S. Government Printing Office, 1914).

_____, *Rules of Land Warfare*, Basic Field Manual. Vol. VII, Pt. II (Washington: U.S. Government Printing Office, 1934).

Army Field Manual No. 27-10, *Rules of Land Warfare* (Washington: U.S. Government Printing Office, 1940).

_____, Revision C1, *Rules of Land Warfare* (Washington: U.S. Government Printing Office, November 15, 1944).

_____, *The Law of Land Warfare* (Washington: U.S. Government Printing Office, July 18, 1956).

_____, Revision C1, *The Law of Land Warfare* (Washington: U.S. Government Printing Office, July 15, 1976).

Army Pamphlet No. 27-1, *Treaties Governing Land Warfare* (Washington: U.S. Government Printing Office, December 7, 1956).

Army Pamphlet No. 27-161-2, *International Law*, Vol. II (Washington: U.S. Government Printing Office, October 23, 1962).

Ayala, Balthazar, *Three Books On the Law of War and On the Duties Connected With War and Military Discipline* (Washington: Carnegie Foundation, 1912).

Aycock, William B. and Seymour W. Wurfel, *Military Law Under the Uniform Code of Military Justice* (Chapel Hill: University of North Carolina Press, 1955).

Bailey, Sydney D., *Prohibitions and Restraints in War* (New York: Oxford University Press, 1972).

Bassiouni, M. Cherif, *A Treatise on International Criminal Law* (Springfield, Ill.: C.C.Thomas, 1973).

_____, and Ved P. Nanda, *International Criminal Law*, Volume I (Springfield: C.C. Thomas, 1973).

Beeler, John, *Warfare in Feudal Europe* (Ithaca, N.Y.: Cornell University Press, 1971).

Belgion, Montgomery, *Victor's Justice* (Chicago: Henry Regnery, 1949).

Belli, Pierino, *A Treatise on Military Matters and Warfare* (Oxford: Clarendon Press, 1936).

Benton, Wilbourn E. and Georg Grimm (eds.), *Nurenberg: German Views of the War Trials* (Dallas: Southern Methodist University Press, 1955).

Biological Testing Involving Human Subjects by the Department of Defense, 1977, Hearings before the Subcommittee on Health and Scientific Research of the Committee on Human Resources, U.S. Senate, 95th Congress, March 8 and May 23, 1977 (Washington: U.S. Government Printing Office, 1977).

Bombing as a Policy Tool in Vietnam: Effectiveness, A Staff Study based on the Pentagon Papers. Prepared for the use of the Committee on Foreign Relations, U.S. Senate Study No. 5 October 12, 1972 (Washington: U.S. Government Printing Office, 1972). Cf. also Study No. 4, *Negotiations, 1964-68: The Half-Hearted Search for Peace in Vietnam* (classified as 'Top Secret').

Bordwell, Percy, *The Law of War Between Belligerents* (Chicago: Callaghan and Company, 1908).

Bosch, William J., *Judgment on Nuremberg: American Attitudes Toward the Major German War-Crimes Trials* (Chapel Hill: University of North Carolina Press, 1970).

Brierly, J.L., *The Law of Nations: An Introduction to the International Law of Peace* (New York: Oxford University Press, 1963).

Burns, Lieutentant-General E.L.M., *Megamurder* (London: George G. Harrap and Company, 1966).

Bynkerschoek, Cornelius von, *Questions of Public Law* (Oxford: Clarendon Press, 1930).

Chemical and Bacteriological (Biological) Weapons and the Effects of Their Possible Use, United Nations Report (New York: Ballantine).

Citizen's Commission of Inquiry (ed.), *The Dellums Committee Hearings on War Crimes in Vietnam* (New York: Random House, 1972).

Clausewitz, Carl von, *On War*, Vols. I,II,III (London: Routledge and Kegan Paul, 1966).

Colbert, Evelyn Speyer, *Retaliation in International Law* (London: King's Crown Press, 1948).

The Committee of Concerned Asian Scholars, *The Indochina Story* (New York: Random House, 1970).

Conot, Robert E., *Justice At Nuremberg* (New York: Harper and Row, 1983).

Cookson, John and Judith Nottingham, *A Survey of Chemical and Biological Warfare* (London: Sheed and Ward, 1969).

Court Martial Reports, Vol. 46, The Judge Advocates General of the Armed Forces of the United States Court of Military Appeals (1971-1973).

Court Martial Reports: Holdings and Decisions of the Courts of Military Review and the United States Court of Military Appeals, Vol. 45, The Judge Advocates General of the Armed Forces and the United States Court of Military Appeals (1971-1972).

Davidson, Eugene, *The Trial of the Germans* (New York: Macmillan, 1966).

Diplomatic Conference for the Establishment of International Conventions for the Protection of Victims of War (Geneva, 1949).

Dubois, Josiah E., *The Devil's Chemists* (Boston: Beacon Press, 1952).

_____, *Generals in Grey Suits* (London: Bodley Head, 1953).

Duffett, John (ed.), *We Accuse! A Report of the Copenhagen Sessions of the War Crimes Trials* (London: Bertrand Russell Peace Foundation, 1968).

_____ (ed.), *Against the Crime of Silence* (New York: Simon and Schuster, 1970).

Falk, Richard A., Gabriel Kolko, and Robert Jay Lifton, *Crimes of War* (New York: Random House, 1971).

Falk, Richard A., *The Status of Law in International Society* (Princeton: Princeton University Press, 1976).

_____ (ed.) *The Vietnam War and International Law* (Princeton: Princeton University Press, 1976).

Fenwick, Charles G., *International Law* (New York: Appleton-Century-Crofts, New York, 1948).

Fraenkel, Ernst, *Military Occupation and the Rule of Law* (New York: Oxford University Press, 1944).

Friedman, Leon (ed.), *The Law of War*. Vols. I and II (New York: Random House, 1972).

Fulbright, William J.,(ed.), *The Vietnam Hearings* (New York: Random House, 1966).

Gautier, Leon, *Chivalry* (New York: Routledge and Sons, 1891).

General Orders 100: Instructions for the Government of Armies of the United States in the Field (Washington: April 24, 1863).

Geneva Conference for the Limitation of Naval Armaments (Geneva: Impremerie Atar, 1927).

Geneva Convention of 1906 for the Amelioration of the Condition of the Wounded Armies in the Field (Washington: Carnegie Foundation, 1916).

Geneva Convention of 1864. Executive Document No. 177, 47th Congress, 1st Session. U.S. Senate (Washington: March 3, 1882).

The Geneva Conventions of August 12, 1949 International Committee of the Red Cross (Geneva, 1949).

Genocide Convention. Hearings Before A Subcommittee of the Committee on Foreign Relations, United States Senate, Ninety-First Congress, April 24, 27, and May 22, 1970 (Washington: 1970).

Genocide Convention. Hearing Before A Subcommittee of the Committee on Foreign Relations, United States Senate, March 10, 1971 (Washington: 1971).

Genocide Convention. Hearings Before The Committee on Foreign Relations, United States Senate, Ninety-Fifth Congress, May 24 and 26, 1977 (Washington: 1977).

Gentili, Alberico, *The Pleas of a Spanish Advocate* (Oxford: Oxford University Press, 1921).

_____, *On the Law of War* (Oxford: Clarendon Press, 1933).

Gershen, Martin, *Destroy or Die: The True Story of Mylai* (New Rochelle: Arlington House, 1971).

Gettleman, Marvin E.(ed.), *Vietnam History, Documents, and Opinions on a Major World Crisis* (New York: Fawcett, 1965).

Gilbert, Gustave M., *The Psychology of Dictatorship* (New York: Ronald Press, 1950).

Glahn, Gerhard von, *Law Among the Nations: An Introduction to Public International Law* (New York: Macmillan, 1970).

Glueck, Sheldon, *War Criminals: Their Prosecution and Punishment* (New York: Alfred A. Knopf, 1944).

Goldstein, Joseph, Burke Marshall, and Jack Schwartz, *The My Lai Massacre and Its Cover-Up: Beyond the Reach of the Law?* (The Peers Commission Report) (New York: The Free Press, 1976).

Greenspan, Morris, *The Modern Law of Land Warfare* (Berkeley and Los Angeles: University of California Press, 1959).

_____, *The Soldier's Guide to the Laws of War* (Washington: Public Affairs Press, 1969).

Grotius, Hugo, *The Law of War and Peace* (Oxford: Clarendon Press, 1925).

Hahn, Walter F. and John C. Neff (eds.), *American Strategy for the Nuclear Age* (New York: Doubleday, 1960).

Haldane, J.B.S., *Callinicus : A Defense of Chemical Warfare* (New York: Garland, 1972).

Hammer, Richard, *One Morning in the War: The Tragedy at Son My* (New York: Coward-McCann, 1970).

Hankey, Lord, *Politics, Trials, and Errors* (Chicago: Henry Regnery, 1950).

_____, *U.N.O. and War Crimes* (London: John Murray, 1951).

Hart, B.H. Liddell, *The Revolution in Warfare* (New Haven: Yale University Press, 1947).

Heydecker, Joe and Johannes Leeb, *The Nuremberg Trials* (London: Heineman, 1962).

Hirsch, Seymour M., *Cover-Up* (New York: Random House, 1972).

Hittle, Lieutenant-Colonel J.D. (ed.), Jomini and His Summary of the Art of War (Harrisburg, Pa.: Military Service Press, 1947).

Hoff, Ebbe Curtis (ed.), *Preventive Medicine in World War II*, Volume IX, Medical Department, U.S. Army, Office of the Surgeon General (Washington: U.S. Government Printing Office, 1969).

Hudson, Manley O., *International Tribunals Past and Future* (Washington: Carnegie Endowment for International Peace, 1944).

Human Drug Testing by the CIA, 1977, Hearings before the Subcommittee on Health and Scientific Research of the Committee on Human Resources, U.S. Senate, 95th Congress, 1st Session, S. 1893, September 20-21, 1977 (Washington: U.S. Government Printing Office, 1977).

The International Military Tribunal, *Trial of the Major War Criminals* (Nuremberg, 1949).

Jackson, Robert H., *The Case Against the Nazi War Criminals* (New York: Alfred A. Knopf, 1946).

Kahn, Herman and Anthony J. Wiener, *The Year 2000* (New York: Macmillan, 1967).

Kahn, Herman, *On Thermonuclear War* (Princeton: Princeton University Press, 1961).

Kalshoven, Frits, *The Law of Warfare: A Summary of Its Recent History and Development* (Leyden: A.A. Sitjhoff, 1973).

Karsten, Peter, *Law, Soldiers, and Combat* (Westport, Conn.: Greenwood Press, 1978).

Keen, Maurice Hugh, *The Law of War in the Late Middle Ages* (London: Routledge and Kegan Paul, 1965).

Keenan, Joseph Berry and Brendan Francis Brown, *Crimes Against International Law* (Washington: Public Affairs Press, 1950).

Kelley, Douglas, *Twenty-Two Cells in Nuremberg: A Psychiatrist Examines the Nazi Criminals* (New York: Greenberg Press, 1947).

Knieriem, August von, *The Nuremberg Trials* (Chicago: Henry Regnery, 1959).

Knoll, Erwin and Judith Nies McFadden, *War Crimes and the American Conscience* (New York: Holt, Rinehart and Winston, 1970).

Kunz, Josef L., *The Changing Law of Nations* (Columbus: Ohio State University Press, 1968).

Lang, Daniel, *Casualties of War* (New York: McGraw Hill, 1969).

The Law of War on Land (London: The War Office, Her Majesty's Stationery Office, 1958).

Law Reports of War Criminals, 15 Vols (London: His Majesty's Stationery Office, 1948).

Legnano, Giovanni da, *Treatise On War* (Oxford: Oxford University Press, 1917).

Lieber, Francis, *Manual of Political Ethics* (Philadelphia: J.B. Lippincott, 1911).

Limqueco, Peter, Peter Weiss, and Ken Coates (eds.), *Prevent the Crime of Silence* (London: Allen Lane, Penguin Press, 1971).

Littauer, Raphael and Norman Upho (eds.), *The Air War in Indochina* (Boston: Beacon Press, 1972).

Marks, John D., *The Search for the Manchurian Candidate: The CIA and Mind Control* (New York: New York Times Books, 1979).

Marshall, S.L.A., *Men Against Fire: The Problem of Battle Command* (Gloucester, Mass.: Peter Smith, 1964).

Martin, Harold H. and Joseph R. Baker (eds), *Laws of Maritime Warfare Affecting Rights and Duties of Belligerents Existing as on August 1, 1914* (Washington: U.S. Government Printing Office, 1918).

Materials on the Trial of Former Servicemen of the Japanese Army Charged With Manufacturing and Employing Bacteriological Weapons (Moscow: Foreign Languages Publishing House, 1950).

McCarthy, Mary, *Medina* (London: Wildwood House, 1973).

McGovern, George, *Vietnam 1976* A Report to the Committee on Foreign Relations, U.S. Senate, March, 1976, 94th Congress, 2nd Session (Washington, 1976).

McNair, Lord and A.D. Watts, *The Legal Effects of War* (Cambridge: Cambridge University Press, 1968).

Mehrish, B.N., *War Crimes and Genocide* (Delhi: Oriental Publishers, 1972).

Melman, Seymour (ed.), *In the Name of America* (Annandale: Turnpike Press, 1968).

Menzel, Paul T. (ed.), *Moral Argument and the War in Vietnam* (Nashville: Aurora Publishers, 1971).

Miale, Florence R. and Michael Selzer, *The Nuremberg Mind* (New York: Quadrangle, 1975).

Midgly, E.B.F., *The Natural Law Tradition and the Theory of International Relations* (London: Paul Elek, 1975).

Milgram, Stanley, *Obedience to Authority* (New York: Harper and Row, 1974).

Minear, Richard H., *Victor's Justice: The Tokyo War Crimes Trial* (Princeton: Princeton University Press, 1971).

Morgan, J.H., *The War Book of the German General Staff* (New York: McBride Nast, 1915).

Moskos, Charles C., Jr., *Peace Soldiers* (Chicago: University of Chicago Press, 1976).

Nazi Conspiracy and Aggression (Washington: U.S. Government Printing Office, 1947).

Neilands, J.B., Gordon H. Orians, E.W. Pfeiffer, Alje Vennema, and Arthur H. Westing, *Harvest of Death: Chemical Warfare in Vietnam and Cambodia* (New York: The Free Press, 1972).

Noel-Baker, Philip John, *The Arms Race: A Program for World Disarmament* (London: Stevens and Sons, 1958).

_____, *The Geneva Protocol for the Pacific Settlement of International Disputes* (London: P.S. King and Sons, 1925).

Oppenheim, L., *International Law: A Treatise* Vol. II. (London: Longmans, 1952).

Pal, Radhabinode, *International Military Tribunal for the Far East: Dissential Judgment* (Calcutta: Sanyal Press, 1953).

Paris, Edmond, *Genocide in Satellite Croatia.1941-1945* (Chicago: The American Institute for Balkan Affairs, 1961).

Patton, George S., *War As I Knew It* (Boston: Houghton-Mifflin, 1947).

Pictet, Jean, *The Principles of International Humanitarian Law* (Geneva: International Committee of the Red Cross, 1966).

Pufendorf, Samuel von, *The Duties of Men and Citizens According to Natural Law* (New York: Oxford university Press, 1927).

_____, *On the Law of Nature and of Nations* (Oxford: Clarendon Press, 1934).

Rachel, Samuel, *Dissertations on the Law of Nature and of Nations* (Washington: Carnegie Foundation, 1916).

Reel, Adolf Frank, *The Case of General Yamashita* (New York: Octagon Books, 1949).

Report of the Conference on Contemporary Problems of the Law of Armed Conflicts. Geneva, September, 1969 (New York, 1971).

Risley, John Shuckburgh, *The Law of War* (London: A.D. Innes. 1952).

Robinson, Frank M. and Earl Kemp, *The Truth about Vietnam* (San Diego: Greenleaf, 1966).

Roling, Bert V.A. and Loga Sukovic, *The Law of War and Dubious Weapons*, Stockholm International Peace Research Institute (Stockholm: Alqvist and Wiksell, 1976).

Rose, Steven (ed.), *CBW: Chemical and Biological Warfare* (London: George G. Harrap and Company, 1968).

Roseburg, Howard L., *Atomic Soldiers: American Victims of Nuclear Experiments* (Boston: Beacon Press, 1980).

Sack, John, *Lieutenant Calley: His Own Story* (New York: Viking Press, 1970).

Schwartzenberger, Georg, *The Legality of Nuclear Weapons* (London: Stevens and Sons, 1958).

Scott, James Brown (ed.), *The Hague Conventions and Declarations of 1899 and 1907* (Oxford: Oxford University Press, 1915).

Seyersted, Finn, *United Nations Forces in the Law of Peace and War* (Leyden: A.W. Sitjhoff, 1956).

Shibata, Shingo, "Lessons of the Vietnam War: Philosophical Considerations on the Philosophical Revolution," *Philosophical Currents*, Vol. 6.

Simmonds, R., *Legal Problems Arising from the United Nations Military Operations in the Congo* (The Hague: Martinus Nijhoff, 1968).

Sleeman, Colin (ed.), *Trial of Gozawa Sadaichi and Nine Others* (London: William Hodge, 1948).

Spaight, J.M., *War Rights on Land* (London: Macmillan, 1911).

Speer, Albert, *Inside the Third Reich,*(tr.) Richard and Clara Winston (New York: Macmillan, 1970).

Stockholm International Peace Research Institute, *The Prevention of CBW,* Vol. 5 of *The Problem of Chemical and Biological Warfare* (Stockholm, 1971).

_____, *The Law of War and Dubious Weapons* (Stockholm: Almqvist and Wiksell, 1971).

Suarez, Francisco, *Selections from Three Works* (Oxford: Clarendon Press, 1944).

Sun Tzu, *The Art of War* (Oxford: Oxford University Press, 1963)

Taylor, Telford, *Final Report to the Secretary of the Army on the Nurenberg War Crimes Trials Under Control Council Law No. 10* (Washington: U.S. Government Printing Office, 1949).

_____, *Grand Inquest* (New York: Ballantine, 1961).

_____, *Nuremberg and Vietnam: An American Tragedy* (New York: Time Books, 1970).

_____, *Sword and Swastika* (New York: Simon and Schuster, 1952).

Technical Manual No. 3-216 and Air Force Manual No. 355-6, *Military Biology and Biological Warfare Agents* (Washington: U.S. Government Printing Office, January 11, 1956).

Textor, Johann Wolfgang, *Synopsis of the Law of Nations* (Washington: Carnegie Foundation, 1916).

Thomas, Ann Van Wynen and A.J. Thomas, Jr., *Legal Limits on the Use of Chemical and Biological Weapons* (Dallas: Southern Methodist University Press, 1970).

Tooke, Joan D., *The Just War in Aquinas and Grotius* (London: S.P.C.K., 1965).

Trials of the Major War Criminals Before the International Military Tribunal, 42 Vols (New York: AMS Press, 1971).

Trials of War Criminals Before the Nuerenberg Military Tribunals Under Control Council Law No. 10, Vol. XV, Nuernberg (October, 1946-April, 1949, Washington: U.S. Government Printing Office.

Troobhoff, Peter D. (ed.), *Law and Responsibility in Warfare: The Vietnam Experience* (Chapel Hill: University of North Carolina Press, 1975).

Twining, Nathan F., *Neither Liberty Nor Safety* (New York: Holt, Rinehart and Winston, 1966).

Union of Anti-Fascist Fighters (eds.), *Criminals On the Bench* (Prague: Orbis Press, 1960).

The United Nations Study on Incendiary Weapons and All Aspects of Their Possible Use, United Nations Document No. A- 8803, October 9, 1972, Cited in *War/Peace Reports* (April, 1973).

Uhl, Michael and Tod Ensign, *G.I. Guinea Pigs: How the Pentagon Exposed Our Troops to Dangers More Deadly than War* (New York: Harper and Row, 1980).

Vattel, Emmerich de, *The Law of Nations or the Principles of Natural Law* (Washington: Carnegie Foundation, 1916).

Verwey, Wil D., *Riot Control Agents and Herbicides in War* (Leyden: A.W. Sitjhoff, 1977).

Victoria, Franciscus de, *On the Indians* (Washington: Carnegie Foundation, 1917).

Vietnam Veterans Against the War (eds.), *The Winter Soldier Investigation: An Inquiry Into American War Crimes* (Boston: Beacon Press, 1972).

Wasserstrom, Richard A., *War and Morality* (Belmont, California: Wadsworth. 1970).

Wehberg, Hans, *The Limitation of Armaments* (Washington: Carnegie Foundation, 1921).

Weisberg, Barry, *Ecocide in Indochina: The Ecology of War* (New York: Canfield Press, 1970).

Wells, Donald A., *The War Myth* (Indianapolis: Bobbs-Merrill, 1967).

Wheaton, Henry, *Elements of International Law* (Oxford: Clarendon Press, 1936).

Wiener, Colonel Frederick Bernays, *The Uniform Code of Military Justice* (Washington: Combat Forces Press, 1950).

Woetzel, Robert K., *The Nuremberg Trials in International Law* (New York: Frederick A. Praeger, 1960).

_____, *The Nuremberg Trials in International Law with a Postlude on the Eichmann Case* (New York: Frederick A. Praeger, 1962).

Wolff, Christian, *The Law of Nations* (Oxford: Clarendon Press, 1934).

World Assembly for Peace, A Report of the meetings in Helsinki, June 22-29, 1955.

Wright, Quincy, *A Study of War* (Chicago: University of Chicago Press, 1962).

Zahn, Gordon C., The Military Chaplaincy: A Study of Role in the Royal Air Force (Toronto: University of Toronto Press, 1969).

Zouche, Richard, *An Exposition of Fecial Law and Procedure, or the Law Between Nations and Questions Concerning the Same* (Washington: Carnegie Foundation, 1911).

INDEX